# PLACES TO HIDE

## IN ENGLAND, SCOTLAND & WALES

DIXE WILLS

ICON BOOKS

Published in the UK in 2006 by
Icon Books Ltd, The Old Dairy,
Brook Road, Thriplow,
Cambridge SG8 7RG
email: info@iconbooks.co.uk
www.iconbooks.co.uk

Sold in the UK, Europe, South Africa and Asia
by Faber & Faber Ltd, 3 Queen Square,
London WC1N 3AU
or their agents

Distributed in the UK, Europe, South Africa and Asia
by TBS Ltd, TBS Distribution Centre, Colchester Road
Frating Green, Colchester CO7 7DW

Published in Australia in 2006
by Allen & Unwin Pty Ltd,
PO Box 8500, 83 Alexander Street,
Crows Nest, NSW 2065

Distributed in Canada by
Penguin Books Canada,
90 Eglinton Avenue East, Suite 700,
Toronto, Ontario M4P 2YE

ISBN-10: 1-84046-768-1
ISBN-13: 978-1840467-68-0

Typesetting and design by
Hands Fotoset, Nottingham

Printed and bound in the UK by
Creative Print and Design Ltd.

*For the lazy sunbathers*

*There is a hiding place in Britain with your name on it.*
*Quite literally. That's the scary thing about them.*

## WARNING

This guide offers you, the reader, a multitude of places in which to hide from the world, society, other people and the worst excesses of what is known, without apparent irony, as civilisation. However, the author would like to make it clear that, however well you hide, the one thing you cannot escape from is yourself. If at any point you discover that you have concealed yourself so well that you no longer know where your self is, you have entered a state known as 'delusion' and should come out immediately with your hands in the air. We are your friends. You can trust us.

———————⟨●⟩———————

## USUAL CAVEAT

If you must injure yourself, whether slightly or mortally, don't do so while hiding at any of the locations featured in this book or while carrying out any of the advice given in these pages. The publishers hereby remind you that you'll receive no sympathy from us and no compensation whatsoever, because whatever calamity has overtaken you was quite clearly your own stupid fault. It's time you started taking responsibility for your actions rather than bleating like a whelpish goat every time a rock-fall in some remote region leaves you pinned to the ground with a shattered pelvis and no means of raising help.

While you're down there, remember that it's probably best not to hide somewhere that belongs to someone (a hateful concept, admittedly, and one day our descendants will chide us for it) because they're almost bound to notice and call your mother.

# TRENDS IN CATEGORISATION

Ever since its adoption in 1932 by the (then named) World Association of Hiders and Concealophiles, the *Loveday-McMillance Standard Classification of Hiding Places* has been the prevailing method of hiding place categorisation throughout the world (exc. Australia), and as such needs no explanation here.

This book conforms to the *Loveday-McMillance* model (exc. p. 103) but, for the sake of completeness, mention should be made of the so-called *Branković Classification* which arranges hiding places by 'Genre', 'Sub-Genre' and 'Nuance' by applying to each of them the Rule of Spatial Irrelevance (the degree to which a place is likely to be overlooked). Conceived in 1982 at the University of Geneva, it owes much of its popularity among the *chatterati* of the hiding scene to the fact that its creators refuse to allow any of it to be translated from the original Latin in which it was written (allegedly as an elaborate, some might say tiresome, inter-faculty joke).

# CONTENTS

# HOW TO USE THIS BOOK

Symbols, numbers, words. All too often in today's post-ironic Britain they can seem but empty husks of inconsequence blown about the threshing floor of meaning by the winds of gloss and style. Not here, however. Here, the loaf of significance is baked in the oven of content and glazed with the milk of substance. Bite ye therefore into it and know that the wheat of knowledge is good.

> 63. MY LIFE IN THE BUSH OF GHOSTS

Love them or loathe them, numbers are probably more than the passing fad they might once have seemed. Here are 62 more to add to the pile – coincidentally, every last one of them an integer. Reassuringly, the name following the number has been proved in tests to describe each hiding place to an accuracy of 1 in 50,000.

**opposite the secret weapons dump, Gloriana, Biffmannockshire**
An address, or something approximating one. Do note, however, that for some years now, counties have been mad things prone to change name or roam the land at the drop of a hat. For instance, in 1983 a disastrous local government ruling led to Yorkshire being entirely subsumed into Sussex in a brand new administrative area called Surk and Yo. The mess took three weeks to sort out, by which time the Yorkshire village of Dourfolk had gone missing altogether, only to be rediscovered in 1996 off the Kent coast when it collided in thick fog with the frigate HMS *Succulent*. For the purposes of this book, the standard used is the 86-county model propounded by the Association of British Counties, a fine upstanding organisation and in no way a second home for people who seek the immediate re-introduction of national service, public floggings, the death sentence, and Roger Whittaker. The only exception to this rule is London's *The Wharf of Death* because, try as one might, one cannot in all seriousness put Southwark and Surrey in the same sentence (this one notwithstanding).

| COASTAL | INSULAR | RURAL | MOUNTAINOUS | URBAN |

A range of pictorial representations of the sort of setting in which the hiding place is to be found. Although useful as a guide, they are not drawn to scale and, where possible, should not be used in lieu of a map.

**RECOMMENDED HIDURATION:** How long might you expect to be able to stay without being discovered/doubling up with cramp/dying of exposure?

**DIMENSIONS:** Will there will be room for your Wurlitzer organ?

**COMFORT:** Judged in ascending order of how plucky you have to be to spend some time there: 1 Plush, 2 Plummy, 3 Pleasant, 4 Placid, 5 Plain, 6 Plebeian, 7 Plangent, 8 Plaguey, 9 Playful, 10 Plath. Category 9 is, sadly, ironic. How you will wish it were not so. Category 10 hiding places are so depressing that they were all destroyed in controlled explosions prior to publication by an NHS Trust set up specifically to make us all feel a bit happier.

**MAP REF:** Some sort of secret code denoting the exact location of the hiding place.

**OS LANDRANGER:** The map on which the hiding place can be found. Available from all good libraries, often behind the large print section or squeezed in next to the periodicals. If in doubt, ask a librarian. She'll be the one with the fringe and the heart-breaking footwear though if only you got to know her you'd find that in her own quiet way she's actually got a lot going for her.

**NEED to KNOW:** All the essential facts, figures, facets and foibles presented in an uplifting style eerily reminiscent of the early work of Floella Benjamin.

**ADVANTAGES:** Situations in which the referee will wave play on.

**HAZARDS:** Ways in which the hiding place is likely to bring about your certain and untimely death.

**ESSENTIALS:**

LOCAL KNOWLEDGE: Knowledge is power. Local knowledge is localised power. Like being a councillor or something.

FREE FOOD: Economists may tell us there's no such thing as a free lunch but, just as in everything else they say about anything, they're entirely wrong. There is in fact no limit to the number of cob nuts and nettles a man or woman can eat and they're all completely free (see **Plant Life and How to Eat It**, p. 106).

SUPPLIES: Contrary to popular belief, there is a limit to the number of cob nuts and nettles a man or woman can eat (this rule does not apply to children, as demonstrated by Edith Sprague in her surprise international bestseller of rural starvation, *My Cob Nut Childhood*), and this is where the concept of 'supplies' enters the dietary equation. This section tells you where to go, how far away that is, and what's on offer when you get there. Don't just eat crisps, though, or your hair will fall out.

PUBLIC CONVENIENCES: Unlike public schools, you will seldom be asked to pay thousands of pounds before entering a public convenience and therein lies their appeal. An essential aid to the amelioration of any mid-to-long-term concealment, the public convenience is the unsung jewel of British civic culture, as anyone who has visited France will tell you.

**OTHER:** We are all searching for the Other. Here it is.

MAKING A QUICK GETAWAY:

Buses, trains and the mysterious Other again. In this instance, the Other takes us from the place where we are to the place we want to be and drops us off there. It's odder than we thought.

COMPROMISED? There is no worse fate for the hider than being found. If you are in imminent danger of having your cover blown, whether literally or metaphorically, this section suggests the nearest or most easily accessible alternative hiding place. If your cover is only going to be blown metaphorically, you would do better to stay put and stop worrying so much about everything.

Each entry concludes with a view of what you can expect to see from the hiding place (or from very near the hiding place if the actual view from the hiding place is grim beyond all description or simply non-existent). Keep in mind that, just like you, views are subject to adverse weather conditions, sudden surges in the rate of sterling, and hangovers.

# AN INTRODUCTION TO HIDING

Too many people think that good hiding is merely a matter of plunging into the depths of the Amazon jungle, constructing a bunker 200 feet down in the Brazilian sod and staying put while breathing shallowly and waiting for the sound of footsteps to die away. However, look up the verb *to hide* in the dictionary and only on very rare occasions will you find Brazil mentioned, even in passing. This is not, as you might think, slackness on the part of the lexicographer, but rather an acknowledgement that concealment from others is a far broader animal than could be expected to launch itself through an average-sized cat flap.

So let us go out into the garden, away from the noise of some creature banging against the back door and squealing as if irretrievably wedged in something, and ponder what it is to hide.

### Centuries of struggle

First, let us be thankful that the days are long gone when a year spent cowering in a ditch disguised as a tree root was seen as no more than a gentleman's duty. Britons today have a much more relaxed attitude towards personal concealment. This can only be good, although it would be a pity to let this new-found openness slide into something approaching complacency. After all, it took centuries of struggle before the masses received the right to vote and now most of us can't be bothered if there happens to be a slight drizzle on polling day.

Before you let hiding go the same way, sit down now and ask yourself the question: 'What about *me* – should *I* hide?' If you responded in the affirmative, read on. If you said 'no', you've got the answer wrong, so go and have another think.

### Lasso

Now that you've established that you *should* hide, the only matter that remains up in the air is just *how* to hide. Lasso that matter in the following three easy steps:

i) Choose a hiding place from the 62 described within these pages.
ii) Read the handy top tips scattered liberally throughout this book. Don't skip the ones you think you might not need, such as basic crouching technique, because knowing you, they'll be exactly the ones you'll have wished you mastered when you find yourself unexpectedly pinned down by police marksmen on Bodmin Moor.
iii) Hide.

It really is that easy.

## Hiding for pleasure

A good many individuals today hide for the sheer pleasure of it. Whether by joining a hide organised by their local branch of the Hiding Association, getting together a few friends for a more informal weekend's hiding, or taking off into the wilds to go to ground *tout seul*, more and more people are recognising the benefits of concealment and live happier, longer lives because of it. Even if you are hiding out of necessity – a state many expert hiders still consider the purest form of the art – there is no reason why you shouldn't still reap the same benefits that so-called 'casuals' derive from the activity. You may not deserve it, but which of us does?

## Hiding for profit

Before you get too excited, it's only fair to point out that only the world's very top hiders are able to make a decent living from practising their craft. Even then, such household names as Guatemala's José 'Muy Muy' Escondido have to make ends meet by spending at least six months of the year hiding for corporate clients. Celtic Icelander Finbar Finsdotterssson frequently appears on charity celebrity quiz shows in which he donates all his winnings to a trust rumoured to be run by his wife; while four-times world champion Tanya Forbes-Elk produces her own range of hiding accessories, Tanya Hide. So, the word is: *Don't* give up your day job, but *do* take time out to hide from it.

## Shameful
Whatever your reasons for hiding, from the innocently quixotic to the shamefully nefarious, let *Places to Hide* be your guide to a lifetime's concealment. To quote the epigram Finsdottersson has made famous throughout the world: 'No matter what you regret in life, you will never regret hiding from it.'

Good be your hiding.

DW
The Yesnaby Battery
Summer 2006

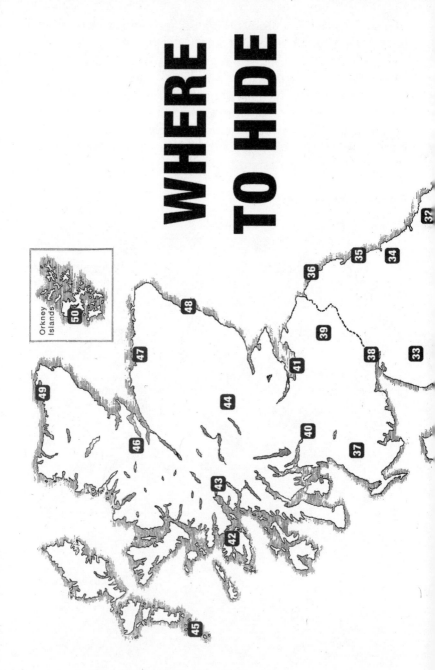

# WHERE TO HIDE

Orkney Islands

50

48

47

49

46

44

41

36

35

34

32

39

38

33

37

40

43

42

45

4

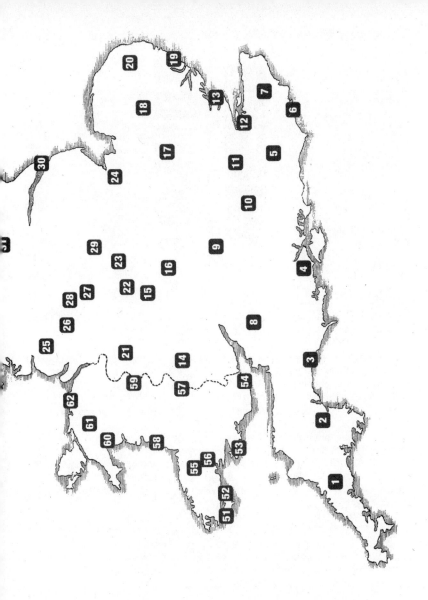

# HIDING IN ENGLAND

*England*

> 'Curse the blasted, jelly-boned swines, the slimy, the belly-wriggling invertebrates, the miserable sodding rotters, the flaming sods, the snivelling, dribbling, dithering, palsied, pulse-less lot that make up England today.'
>
> *D.H. Lawrence, in a letter to Edward Garnett, July 1912*

And this was Lawrence's summation of the English *before* they accused him of being in league with the Germans. However, as we all know, the sons and daughters of Albion can't possibly have been as bad as all that back in the time of George V. For instance, could such a nation as that drawn by Lawrence have been capable of spawning the inventor of the umbrella? Didn't think of *that*, did he?

Even today, the English do not live up to all of the great man's epithets and for this they must thank the country into which they have been born, for it is one of dazzling possibilities both to the hider and the casual *ephemeriste* alike. Barely a river runs through it that does not throw up an ox-bow lake of opportunity for concealment; hardly an office block is built that does not yield up some corner forever in deepest shade.

Despite this, or perhaps because of it, the country remains something of an enigma, even to its own people. For instance, the mistake most often made about England by the English – aside from the belief that its football team will one day sweep all before it to claim the World Cup again – is that the country is somehow made up of just one homogenous lump of matter: that a cubic foot of Cumbria is much the same as a similar quantity of Devon.

This false assertion has grown in popularity largely thanks to the free market, that cancerous lumbering death that has rendered 90 per cent of English town centres indistinguishable from each other. However, it is still abundantly clear that, once the High Street has been left behind, a visitor could no more mistake one region for another than confuse Troilus for Cressida, even if both were being played by Brian Blessed in a one-man show touring the very regions whose distinctiveness has been called into question in so unseemly a manner. For this reason, it is a matter of civic duty to highlight the diversity of each region and how it might affect you.

### The south-west
First there is Cornwall, a Celtic outpost that has been annexed by the English but which one day will be free again. More germane to our purposes, it is as holey as a string vest and thus lends itself to the talents of the speleological hider. The rest of the south-west is made up of counties that are basically large green blankets that can be pulled over one's head at a moment's notice.

### The south-east
This is an area consisting entirely of people. So thickly populated is the region that the ground beneath the inhabitants has not been seen since 1982. Hiding here therefore is more a question of disguising yourself as a south-easterner and being borne along by the ebb and flow of bodies until such time as it is safe to leave.

### East Anglia
A place of fens, gravel pits, hundred-foot drains and Norwich. A challenge but a rewarding one.

### The Midlands
A conurbation of no specific purpose stretching roughly from Dudley to Leicester. Note particularly the famous crags of Nuneaton behind which a sizeable band of Royalist soldiers fleeing the Battle of Naseby is still known to be in hiding.

### The north-west
A mixture of heavy industry and the Lake District. Also contains Blackpool, a town whose description is still not possible in the English language.

### The north-east
Once an industrial wasteland, government funding has enabled the north-east to transform itself into a post-industrial wasteland. Thankfully, this has been achieved without sacrificing any of the niches, recesses and depressions that industrial wastelands afford the hider. Highly recommended.

# 1. ALL MINE

nr Minions, Bodmin Moor, Cornwall

**NEED TO KNOW:** Far enough out on Bodmin Moor to spare you from scrutiny by whatever passing trade the wind might blow into the vicinity, this former Phoenix United Mine engine house was once instrumental in the hoovering up of tin and copper deposits. It might also be worth your while to know that Cornwall isn't in England at all, and do not make the mistake of claiming it is so, should you happen to meet a Cornish person (they're the pitiful beings you'll see roaming the streets peering longingly through the windows of the second homes of upper-middle-class couples from London).

**ADVANTAGES:** An emergency secondary hiding place – the less imaginative might call it a hole – can be found just by the pond that supplies the former engine house with water. Furthermore, lush views of the Cheesewring quarry and the massed aerials of Caradon Hill ensure there's rarely a dull moment.

**HAZARDS:** Should you alight on a dull moment, you can always chase it away with thoughts of the Beast of Bodmin, an animal that has been known to devour whole villages in a single bite, leaving a sort of awkward gap in the landscape and creating more work for the boys and girls at the Ordnance Survey.

**ESSENTIALS:**

LOCAL KNOWLEDGE: The Hurlers, a curtsy away to the east, are three rather impressive circles of standing stones. As is de rigueur for such sites, they turn out to be the petrified forms of individuals who desecrated the Sabbath – in this case by playing the ancient Celtic game of hurling (a sort of rugby without the subtleties). So many people desecrated the Sabbath in years gone by that it was all God could do to keep up. In the end, He gave it up as a bad job and we've been reaping the whirlwind ever since.

**FREE FOOD:** The roots of reeds growing in the ponds nearby make a tasty snack if you can cook them right. Furthermore, the canes, if punctured, exude a sort of edible gum which I suppose you could eat on alternate days for a bit of variety.

**SUPPLIES:** Minions Village Shop and Tea Rooms (0.6 miles), at 995 feet above sea level, is the highest shop in Cornwall.

**PUBLIC CONVENIENCES:** The highest ones in Cornwall, right next to the Hurlers Halt tea rooms (0.6 miles).

**IF IT ALL GETS TOO MUCH:** The Cheesewring Hotel (0.6 miles) is the highest inn in Cornwall. You may start to notice a pattern developing here.

**RECOMMENDED HIDURATION:**
3–4 days

**DIMENSIONS:**
5m x 11m

**COMFORT:**
4 Placid

**MAP REF:**
SX 253 712

**OS LANDRANGER:** 201

## MAKING A QUICK GETAWAY:

**TRAIN:** The Liskeard and Caradon Railway used to run past here. A ride from Liskeard onto the moors was a favourite Sunday School outing in Victorian times. Not any more, I'm afraid, so you'll have to walk. People think it's just a form of travel that is lost when a railway dies but actually it's a whole culture. So now you know.

## COMPROMISED?
Try 2. *The End of Stone Row* (40 miles).

*Occasionally the world here may seem to turn on its side. This is just a trick the locals play on unwary tourists. If anyone in a pub offers you 'some nice trousers just your size', decline them politely but firmly.*

9

# 2. THE END OF STONE ROW

**Cosdon Hill, Dartmoor, Devon**

**NEED TO KNOW:** 'Je suis partout', as Kafka so wittily put it in his poem. You, however, are not everywhere, which is just as well because it is ferociously difficult to hide yourself when you are. In fact, if you find it difficult to limit your body to a size equal to or less than 1m x 2m, the stone row at Cosdon Hill might not be the place for you. If, on the other hand, folk are constantly remarking that your svelte frame makes them feel, in comparison, like a mammoth crossed with some unspecified dinosaur of their own imagining, you should seriously consider making a permanent move here. Simply slip your lissom form behind one or other stone at the end of the row and disappear from the world. Should the world appear from the side on which you're hiding, wait until it's looking the other way, then steal around the other side like the wispy shadow you are.

**ADVANTAGES:** Any tenant can expect to be able to lodge here indefinitely in times of fog. Happily, these are most times. On non-foggy days you'll just have to do the best you can with Dartmoor's only other weather form, impenetrable layers of mist.

**HAZARDS:** Being nothing more substantial than a will-o'-the-wisp inside the apparent solidity of a great wall of fog can cause a certain mental instability known to psychiatrists as *Simpkin's Unpresent Disorder*, the effects of which can be disastrous to the sufferer, if amusing to onlookers.

**ESSENTIALS:**

**LOCAL KNOWLEDGE:** Given that average life expectancy during the Bronze Age was about twenty, most people who were born then have now left us. This fine example of a triple stone row leads to the last resting place of one of them, presumably an eminent one or, at the very least, a minor celeb with his own cookery show or some such.

**FREE FOOD:** Of which, you look like you could probably do with a good square meal, which is a pity because there's pitifully little around here from which to rustle one up. I can only suggest you bring plentiful supplies with you, or find some way of digesting grass.

**SUPPLIES:** Chris, Helen and family welcome you to The Store in South Zeal (1.4 miles), everything a village-shop-cum-post-office should be. Also, they absolutely promise not to give the game away if you are immoderately lissom and enquire as to the availability of books dealing with the digestion of grass.

**RECOMMENDED HIDURATION:**
8–12 hours

**DIMENSIONS:**
1m x 2m

**COMFORT:**
6 Plebeian

**MAP REF:**
SX 643 916

**OS LANDRANGER:** 191

## MAKING A QUICK GETAWAY:

**BUS:** The X9 – more properly a name for a weapon imparting instant death than a bus, though sometimes they're the same thing – takes the slender and rounded alike to Bude, Exeter and Okehampton from a stop in Ramsley (1 mile).

COMPROMISED? Try *3. Household in the Hills* (37 miles).

*Have horse, will stay more or less in the same place.*

# STARTING OUT

The waves crash against the disintegrating pier of your indecision. A theatre that once rang to improbable applause aimed at Max Wall burns down and the Irresolution Police point the finger at you. A man who used to cut your hair now injects cheap lager into his knees – he lies unconscious in the gutter of your prevarication.

Thankfully, it needn't always be like this when starting out in the big bold world of hiding. Faced by the unrelenting social pressure not just to hide, or even to hide well, but to hide *the best*, the most competent of us can crack, so what has happened to you is really no disgrace.

What you have to remember is that hiding is really a lot less complicated than your so-called friends would have you believe (indeed, it needn't even be competitive). Many people derive a great deal of joy from simply hiding for fun or to kill time between acting jobs. The trick is not to be daunted by the intimidating giraffe that society has made of The Art of Hiding but to break it down into its constituent parts. Who but a child, for instance, could be frightened of a giraffe's aorta?[1]

In a nutshell, there are three basic elements to hiding.

1. The Hider
2. The Hiding Place
3. Time

Address each of these as individual entities and then fit them together as you might an Airfix model of a Spitfire Mark Ia or the matching accessories of a Cindy doll and, hey presto, you're hiding.

**1. The Hider**
Always check first that it is you who is intending to hide and not i) a random acquaintance, ii) the farmer whose barn you accidentally converted into two luxury loft apartments while on holiday last summer but who was remarkably good about it considering, or iii) your imaginary friend, Biff. If it is you, cement this fact in some way, perhaps by scratching the word 'hider' on your arm with a fountain pen. This will make you feel really in command of the situation and ready to face the second hurdle:

**2. The Hiding Place**
With experience, even the beginner can turn unpropitious hiding circumstances into first-rate places of concealment. A shallow fissure in a cliff face

---

[1] Actually, giraffes have the largest hearts of any land mammal so their aortas are pretty scary things even when encountered in isolation but it's probably best not to think about this just yet.

*'Fit them together as you might an Airfix model of a Spitfire Mark Ia.'*

can become a cave; three twigs, a sheltering thicket. King George III famously hid for three weeks in a pea-pod – a feat that all but precipitated a constitutional crisis. In the meantime, it might be best to practise at home with a friend and a door.

### 3. Time

What is time but the device by which we measure events passing? Even the fact that God is said to exist outside of time is no reason to despair since that will always be more his concern than yours, although of course what 'always' means in a state of timelessness is itself open to question, as is – I suppose some people might quibble – the existence of God. If you're of the latter party (the quibblers, that is, not God), you'll just have to have faith that time created itself. Either way, unless something quite unusual happens, you can more or less rely on time just getting on with it.

Now all you have to do is work backwards and put them all together.

3. Locate yourself somewhere within the space-time continuum.
2. Hide.
1. Check your arm. If you can read the word 'hider' you are now successfully concealing yourself. If not, you'll probably find your imaginary friend Biff has gone missing. Try to join him.

# 3. HOUSEHOLD IN THE HILLS

nr Ryall, Dorset

**NEED to KNOW:** That Geoffrey Household was a tease (see p. 114). Read his posh-outdoors-type-takes-on-dodgy-foreign-power-but-ends-up-hiding-in-a-muddy-burrow-in-Dorset-with-a-dead-cat novel *Rogue Male* (see p. 114 again – in fact, put your finger in the page this time) and you'll get no more than a few vague clues as to where the foetid den in question actually was. There is mention of the Marshwood Vale, the village of Whitchurch Canonicorum and an ancient lane that is, rather conveniently, 'not marked on the map'. A deep sandstone lane apparently crosses another at right angles. This latter pathway leads to the north and branches into two farm tracks. You have to ignore these and plough on over a field. Here there is a thick hedge in which the lane reappears. Not much to go on really, particularly if you don't know the location of the deep sandstone lane you're meant to have started from. In the end you just feel a bit foolish and wish you'd never come out at all, especially as it looks like it's coming on to rain (to avoid getting caught in the rain in future, see **Using the Weather**, p. 208).

**ADVANTAGES:** Going by the pointers in Household's book, this may well have been the place. It certainly ticks most of the boxes, and the unticked ones can, rather conveniently, be put down to changes in the landscape in the decades since the yarn was first published. The hidey-hole therefore has all the advantages of the one described in the novel except for the fact that you will have to dig out the burrow again. Sandstone is one of the easier rocks though, in this regard, so chin up.

**HAZARDS:** Like the lair-in-the-midst-of-a-hedge portrayed by the author, this one is on a farm. His hero, being fictional, found it unnecessary to ask the equally fictitious farmer's permission to spend the entire summer underground on his land. You, however, belong to the world of non-fiction, as does the farmer, as you will discover if you attempt a similar feat.

## ESSENTIALS:

**LOCAL KNOWLEDGE:** 'At present I exist only in my own time, as one does in a nightmare, forcing myself to a fanaticism of endurance. Without a God, without a love, without a hate – yet a fanatic! An embodiment of that myth of foreigners, the English gentleman, the gentle Englishman. I will not kill; to hide I am ashamed. So I endure without object.' Blimey.

**FREE FOOD:** Blackberries when in season, otherwise the hills are a bit rabbit-cropped to provide much in the way of sustenance.

**SUPPLIES:** Moore's Dorset Biscuits in Morcombelake (1.3 miles) features all the usual victuals you would expect from a biscuit shop, including Moore's Experimental Chocolate Chip biscuits, Elizabethan saffron cake, bottled lentils, and sea beans in brine.

**PUBLIC CONVENIENCES:** No right-minded novelist suggests that a hero/ine has such base bodily functions. Take a leaf out of their book and just hold it in.

**COMPROMISED?** Try *8. Royal Crescent Garden* (49 miles).

*A pity, really, because the view beyond is lovely.*

# 4. THE NEW FOREST CHÂTEAU

**Bolderford Bridge, nr Brockenhurst, Hampshire**

**NEED to KNOW:** Lock a group of 50 experienced hiders in a tiny room and refuse to let them out until they have agreed on a 'top five' of geological features they like to have near at hand when hiding, and there's a good chance that the foetid scrap of paper they hand you a month later will include 'a confluence of rivers' at number three. For that reason alone, this qualifies as a choice venue, for here Highland Water, Blackwater and Ober Water combine with a commendable lack of fuss to form the Lymington River. Constructed of bricks, mortar, mysterious metal conduits and a strange kind of upside-down test tube affair, the *Château* (lit. 'cat water') may once have had something to do with drainage in a dim and unbearably distant past. It has a (non-identical) twin twenty yards away that undoubtedly functioned as something at some point as well and may still do so (as a rule, it's best not to delve too assiduously into the secrets of the forest).

**ADVANTAGES:** Tucked away among the trees, you are unlikely to be pestered by trippers, walkers, cyclists or any of the ponies, red, roe, sika, muntjac and fallow deer that amble around the forest as if they owned the place. Amateur poets, word enthusiasts and other sundry linguaphiles might also enjoy eating Black Forest gateau here.

**HAZARDS:** Beneath the comforting patina of leaf mulch there lies a perma-bog of alluvial sludge. Bring snow shoes or a belief in the curative values of total sludge immersion. Also, once a year the locals claim ancient right of Pannage, the letting loose of hundreds of pigs into the forest to graze on the acorns that might otherwise poison the ponies. These pigs are essentially harmless but can be roused to violence by an impassioned speech from any of their more politicised fellows or the smell of freshly disturbed alluvial sludge.

## ESSENTIALS:

**LOCAL KNOWLEDGE:** Aside from Pannage, the populace round about also enjoys the rights of Common (grazing of ponies, cattle, sheep and donkeys), Turbary (cutting of turf or peat) and Marl (digging limy clay). By exercising your ancient right of Cower (hiding inside a brick building wearing snow shoes) you step into the flow of English history.

**FREE FOOD:** Primroses and dandelions abound – a joy not only to the vase and eye but the plate and palate too.

**SUPPLIES:** A tiny ice cream trailer at the Rhinefield Arboretum (2 miles) sells locally made ices in three sizes. Otherwise, there's Streets the ironmonger in Brockenhurst (2.5 miles) for uni-sized millet and onion sets.

**PUBLIC CONVENIENCES:** Also at the arboretum. In case you were wondering, millet is something of a general term that covers any of a number of cereal plants. Only cereal farmers have any real interest in distinguishing between them.

**RECOMMENDED HIDURATION:**
6–8 hours

**DIMENSIONS:**
2m x 2.5m

**COMFORT:**
7 Plangent

**Map ref:**
SU 292 042

**OS LANDRANGER:** 196

**COMPROMISED?** Try *10. Bagshot by Both Sides* (55 miles).

*The sort of Nature-meets-Drainage beauty that you feel Constable would have made a bit of a hash of.*

17

# BUILDING YOUR OWN HIDING PLACE

Some places in Britain – we shall name names in a moment – are blatantly very far from conducive to the art of concealment. The vast open plains of Lincolnshire, for instance; the Sahara-like expanses of Goodwin Sands; the seemingly limitless salt flats of Berkshire[1] – none of these afford the hider anything like enough protection from the gaze of an all too curious public. The sheer barrenness of such regions may be reason enough for the fainter of heart to abandon them in favour of more fertile territories such as the Thousand Acre Wood of Clapham; the dark glaciers of Newton Abbot; and Scotland. However, this would be a pity since the very improbability of a person choosing to hide in some exposed district makes it all the less likely a target for search parties. All that is then required to vouchsafe many weeks of contented seclusion is to fashion a simple refuge.

Take, if you will, the dry stone wall corral. Although even the humblest examples of these are famously difficult to transport, by apprising oneself of the basic method of construction, one need never be more than half an hour or so from safety, comfort, and most importantly, privacy.

*'Nope. We've lost him.'*

[1] A trick of the light – they actually end just outside Reading.

### i) Tools
You will need: a spade, some pegs, some string (one ball, roughly the size of a half-grown Indonesian spittle fruit), a 4lb club hammer, a crowbar, a mallet, a cold chisel, a plank of varying length and some rope. If you do not have these to hand, do your best to fashion them from the materials at your disposal. For example, with a little patience your hair can be made into a serviceable rope (avoid the schoolboy error of neglecting to detach it first).

### ii) Rocks
No dry stone wall is complete without rocks. The best place to find them, naturally, is in a shop. Failing this, look for them where a rocky substrate lies close to the surface. Failing that, any rock-strewn landscape will do. Failing *this* and *that*, you should bring your own. (If you do bring your own, do not stint: inflatable rocks may be lighter and more wieldy but they are no substitute for the real thing.)

### iii) The circle
Mark out the limits of your corral with pegs and string. A diameter equivalent to your own body length is ideal, though if you are planning a lengthy sojourn within, you may wish to add an extra couple of inches all round for toiletries, personal effects and perhaps the odd eye-pleasing ornament (a blown-glass goat, perhaps, or if you wish to make more of a political statement, the dove of peace made out of spent cartridge shells). If you lack the artist's natural talent for drawing a perfect circle freehand, it is no shame to use a large pair of compasses.

### iv) Foundation
This needn't be a lavish affair. Dig an 8-inch trench round your pegged-out circle. This may not seem much, and as a consequence it is easy to get carried away 'just to be on the safe side', but remember that you are not creating a moat. Nor will there be extra prizes if your dry stone wall is still standing in 2,000 years' time.

### v) The wall
The trick is to lay two parallel lines of stones sort of leaning in towards each other. 'Tapering' is the technical term but consider yourself to have done well if 'sort of leaning' is as close as you get. Every few feet you should employ tie-in stones, if you know what they are. If not, don't worry – the inevitable collapse of your untied-in wall is sure to look spectacular. Finally, do remember to build the corral from the inside. There are few more heart-rending sights than that of a would-be hider who has inadvertently built himself out of his own haven.

*'More or less anything hard and lumpy that can be arranged in some kind of order will do.'*

## vi) Alternative building materials

Some materials make an excellent stand-in for rocks. As a rule of thumb, more or less anything hard and lumpy that can be arranged in some kind of order will do. In no event should you be tempted to use things that just look like rocks, such as gall stones, liquorice cuttings or sleet.

# SCENES FROM THE WORLD OF SECLUSION

## nr *30. Some Sort of Building*

*Extreme Military Architecture No. 4: Contrary to popular belief, this subterranean pill-box has actually been rising up out of the sand since World War II. In twenty years' time it will be airborne.*

# 5. EEYORE'S GLOOMY PLACE

Gill's Lap, Ashdown Forest, Sussex

**NEED to KNOW:** If two beech trees fall in the forest, does anybody hear? If somebody were to hear, but mistook the crash for another common woodland sound like, say, that of an otter falling off a tricycle, would the ramifications really be so terrible? The evidence on the slopes of *Eeyore's Gloomy Place* is that they would not, since here two fallen beech trees have combined to produce a hiding place of the first order, their upturned roots forming the entrance to a snug little warren of which Rabbit himself would have been proud. Combine this with the fact that A.A. Milne placed Eeyore – the donkey who introduced the concept of clinical depression to generations of infants the world over – in this otherwise unremarkable valley, and you have the makings of a very exceptional *endroit caché* indeed.

**ADVANTAGES:** If you find yourself becoming somewhat lachrymose while installed here, you can at least console yourself with the thought that, unlike a donkey, you have an opposable thumb.

**HAZARDS:** The Ashdown Forest, for all its homely associations, is a nest of danger built by the rooks and crows of impending hazard. If the falling trees don't get you, be assured that the forest fires or the adders will. Your only hope is to make for a pond and hope that the falling trees miss you and land instead on any adders that might have designs on turning your leg into a flute.

**LOCAL KNOWLEDGE**: A.A. Milne died 50 years ago. E.H. Shepard died 30 years ago. Winnie-the-Pooh lives on in all our hearts. Discuss with reference to the trite colonisation of spirituality by Hollywood scriptwriters.

**FREE FOOD**: Beech nuts, here in plentiful supply, are not solely used in the manufacture of chewing gum, as is often believed. They also make for an appetising and nutritious snack that, like chewing gum, won't fill you up between meals or, sadly, in lieu of them.

**SUPPLIES**: In summer, an ice cream van at Gill's Lap car park should meet any gelid lactic needs you may have, but remember that a trail of impru-

dently dripped milk, vegetable oils and vanilla essence has led to the discovery of more than one fugitive whose hideaway was otherwise sleuth-proof. In spring, autumn and winter, drip towards Forest Row (3 miles).

**FOOD FOR THOUGHT**: 'Good morning, Pooh Bear', said Eeyore gloomily. 'If it is a good morning', he said. 'Which I doubt.'

| |
|---|
| **RECOMMENDED HIDURATION:** 2 days |
| **DIMENSIONS:** 1.5m x 1.5m x 2m (high) |
|  **COMFORT:** 6 Plebeian |
| **MAP REF:** TQ 474 322 |
| **OS LANDRANGER:** 188 |

## MAKING A QUICK GETAWAY :

**BUS**: Rumour has it that an East Sussex County Council tourist bus passes here in the summer. Enjoy the wait.

COMPROMISED? Try 12. *The Wood at the Foot of the Stairs* (31 miles).

*The more it snows (Tiddly Pom) the colder you're likely to be.*

# 6. THE CLIFFS, THE CLIFFS

below Hastings Castle, West Hill Cliffs, Hastings, Sussex

**NEED TO KNOW:** Hastings may not be the site of the Battle of Hastings (that honour falls to the village of Battle – presumably they thought it would sound ridiculous to call history's most memorable clash the Battle of Battle) but it's got Underwater World and Smugglers Adventure and cliff lifts and everything. Of course, 'a cliff lift without a cliff is like a headmaster without a head', to quote the old saw, and so it is a relief to report that Hastings is not lying dead in its office, bleeding over the end-of-term reports and unable to take the junior assembly. These cliffs being of sandstone, the so-called 'thoughtful mineral', they have taken pains to erode themselves in ways conducive to hiding. Thus, just below the plucky remains of Hastings Castle, there is found a cranny of which Gaudí himself would have been proud.

**ADVANTAGES:** Bird's eye views of the crazy golf course and go-karting circuit mean that fans of hilarious putter-related hi-jinks and the gratuitous depletion of the ozone layer will go home happy.

**HAZARDS:** The local yoof are in the habit of congregating just below here at weekends to perform the age-old pre-courtship rituals of chasing each other around, drinking illicitly purchased beverages, and squealing. Although they are unlikely to bother you (local by-laws prohibit under-18s from chasing with intent to cause squealing at heights greater than 100 feet above sea level), it's best to know that they are there in case you begin to imagine that the incessant shrieking and yapping from down below is the external manifestation of the turbulence wracking your troubled soul.

## ESSENTIALS:

**LOCAL KNOWLEDGE:** An Irish family is reputed to have lived in the East Hill caves for several years. This was, of course, back in the days when the so-called 'cave tourism' craze was at its zenith. This caused such depopulation in Ireland that for six months no one could be found to sit on the Dublin City Council and it was run almost entirely by sheep and (briefly) a haddock.

**FREE FOOD:** Anything that drops here from a gull's mouth is likely to be unhygienic so do make sure you wash it first.

**SUPPLIES:** The café near the cliff lift is full of tea.

**RECOMMENDED HIDURATION:**
2–3 days

**DIMENSIONS:**
10m x 1m x 3m

**COMFORT:**
2 Plummy

**MAP REF:**
TQ 821 094

**OS LANDRANGER:** 199

**PUBLIC CONVENIENCES:** Just 100 yards away, next door to the cliff lift (or the West Hill Cliff Railway (summer 10am – 5.30pm, winter 11am – 4pm) as it prefers, as if such pomposity did not make it the subject of ridicule from Dungeness to Bexhill).

## MAKING A QUICK GETAWAY:

**TRAIN:** A miniature railway speeds passengers along the sea front from nowhere in particular to nowhere much at all – both highly prized destinations in the world of the hider – for a pound a go.

**COMPROMISED?** Try 5. *Eeyore's Gloomy Place* (28 miles).

*The game that put the K into Crazy.*

# CHOOSING A PSEUDONYM

Very often, in the run up to a period of disappearance, it is desirable to take on board a *nom de plume* or two. These might typically be used (one at a time, mind) at a guest house in the Highlands, say, the night before you burrow into a leith for the winter; or when booking a train ticket to a town rich in hiding potential but also known to be a sanctuary for desperados and excommunicants (Pontefract is an obvious example, but a surprising number of settlements in Buckinghamshire also fit the bill[1]).

The selection of the correct name for you is of paramount importance if you really want to throw your pursuers off the scent. Don't make the classic mistake of using your mother's maiden name (the so-called 'Bank Question' error), your own name in reverse order (the 'Second O'First' howler) or the surname of your husband's mistress (known in the trade as 'doing an Agatha' – see p. 38).

To help you take your first steps towards that special *nom de guerre* that will make you the envy of your pals and otherwise close-knit family, study the following suggestions and try out a combination the next time you need to go 'General Tito' as our Cockney friends have it.

'Charles King'
(See? It fools no one.)

[1] A full list of such towns can be obtained from the British Red Cross.

| First Name | | Surname | |
|---|---|---|---|
| **Sebastian** | Goes best with a look that says: 'I'm dressing down today – on the estate I wear nothing but tweed.' | **Smith** | Something of a cliché but useful in a dire emergency. For variation, try employing it as a first name. |
| **David/Dave** | *David*: Solid, dependable, slightly dull.<br>*Dave*: Wild, good for a laugh, drug dealer. Make sure you know which one you are purporting to be before you leave the house. | **Jones** | Do not attempt accompanying inflections unless actually Welsh. Likely to arouse suspicion if coupled with 'Tom' or 'Bridget'. |
| **Jo/Joe** | Demonstrative, would-be actor, conversant with modern techniques in the production of cheese. | **Clark/ Clarke** | Common, but less likely to raise an hotelier's matronly eyebrow. Make sure to correct her spelling of Clark/e regardless of the one she has gone for. |
| **Sophie** | A gentle manner, perhaps a hint of lace, prone to the composition of poetry re the plight of the gerbil. | **Black** | A surname that says: 'Don't ask questions.' Particularly effective if preceded by 'Dr'. |
| **Svetlana** | If you can do the accent, absolutely unstoppable. | **Balderkin-Piffleshmertz** | All-stops-out eccentricity means it is unlikely to be challenged but may draw unwanted attention to yourself. Use sparingly. |

# 7. THE CLEARING

**Broad Down, nr Wye, Kent**

**NEED TO KNOW:** Shielded from easterly winds and the attentions of the overly curious by an almost unbroken screen of beech and hawthorn shrubs. Although open to the vicissitudes of the sky, it should be remembered that human skin is for the most part impermeable and that any infelicitous drizzle, rain, sleet, cats/dogs etc. that fall on the ground around the occupant will drain swiftly away through the chalk beneath.

**ADVANTAGES:** A floor of woody detritus provides a pleasantly yielding vantage point from which to take in views across the Kent Weald to the South Downs. The generous living space and lack of roof make *The Clearing* eminently suitable for the claustrophobic hider for whom a wardrobe spells terror.

**HAZARDS:** Although the beech and hawthorn barrier guarantees protection from snoopers, it may not prove failsafe against snipers. If you feel there is any danger that you might be the target of the latter you are advised to wear some body armour or to keep moving about. Guard dogs howling in the valley below can be unnerving at night but rest assured that it will probably put the snipers off just as much as they fumble with their night-sights and infra-red pinpointing devices.

**ESSENTIALS:**

**LOCAL KNOWLEDGE:** Wye Brides, in Wye (1.5 miles) are stockists of Alfred Angelo bridal wear. This may come in very useful should a dramatic change of appearance suddenly become desirable.

**FREE FOOD:** Hawthorn berries; field mushrooms; water mint – not exactly food but the oil from same is very good for those with indigestion, perhaps brought on by a sleepless night eating raw hawthorn berries.

**SUPPLIES:** A perfectly adequate mediumish super-market in Wye, of the co-operative variety.

**PUBLIC CONVENIENCES:** Opposite St Gregory and St Martin's Church, Wye.

**PUBLIC LIBRARY:** Also in Wye, which turns out to be something of a metropolis. Open sketchily on Tues/Thurs/Fri/Sat.

**RECOMMENDED HIDURATION:**
Up to 24 hours

**DIMENSIONS:**
30m x 4m

**COMFORT:**
4 Placid

**MAP REF:**
TR 077 453

**OS LANDRANGER:** 189

## MAKING A QUICK GETAWAY:

**BUS:** Services to Ashford and Canterbury (nine a day), and Tenterden (just the once – school term time only).

**TRAIN:** Ashford International is a single stop away from Wye station. From there, direct trains to the Continent can be boarded. Police evidence suggests that very few hitmen will bother to travel abroad to carry out their contracts.

**OTHER:** If you have thought to bring along a hang-glider, now is the time to use it.

## COMPROMISED? Try 6. The Cliffs, The Cliffs (30 miles).

*The Kent Weald, a name derived from the Old English 'Kent wald' meaning 'a place whereof the otter speaketh not, nor neither doth the stoat, nor the weasel – notwithstanding that he be weasely recognised – nor durst any creature that slippeth and slideth through the water, neither the male nor the female of the same, nor their offspring be they exceeding runtish etc. etc.'.*

# 8. ROYAL CRESCENT GARDEN

just off Royal Avenue, just below Royal Crescent, Bath, Somerset

**NEED TO KNOW:** John Wood Jr was largely responsible for Bath's pride and joy, the Royal Crescent, though his father (who whipped up the Royal Circus just along the road) had a hand in it before dying (presumably of hand poisoning or something). The elegant Palladian curve of golden Bath stone took eight years to build, which seems a long time somehow for a row of terraced houses. Anyway, more to the point, the greensward below has remained untrammelled by the insensible boot of the builder, and the gardens provide excellent concealment opportunities even in the depths of winter, there being a goodly spread of evergreens among the fair-weather vegetation.

**ADVANTAGES:** For full protection from the wandering eyes of hoi polloi, you'll need to venture into the deep cover beyond the japonica, box, holly, laurel and so forth towards the back of the *Royal Crescent Garden* where the proper trees begin. Once there, your view of the Crescent, though of necessity framed by fir, is second to few.

**HAZARDS:** Bath can become a tad overrun in the summer with people only too keen to misquote the opening sentence of *Pride and Prejudice*. Lamentably, this is a state of affairs liable to continue into the foreseeable future unless some sort of system of penalties is introduced by the town council (£500 for a first offence, say, rising to 'death from a chill caught whilst out riding in a storm' for persistent offenders).

**ESSENTIALS:**

**LOCAL KNOWLEDGE:** It's a terrible irony, but Jane Austen really didn't care for Bath. She lived there for five years but wrote to her sister Cassandra that she left with 'happy feelings of Escape!' Perhaps this was because, back in 1806, Bath was yet to be moulded in her image. Having said that, what would it be like to live in a town dedicated to your memory? Fun at first, I imagine, then strangely cloying.

**FREE FOOD:** Bathians live on an exclusive diet of tea and Madeira cake so it's possible that you might find the odd crumb that has strayed from a bone-china side plate, or the leaves from a surreptitiously emptied pot of Earl Grey.

**SUPPLIES:** A tiny anonymous old-school green-grocer on Julian Road (0.3 miles) where the owners share an unwarranted scepticism about Stanley Baldwin's handling of the abdication and cast fear-ful glances across to Germany where the Chancellor appears to be rousing the rabble into an unfortunate pitch of excitement. Bring old money.

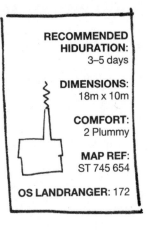

**RECOMMENDED HIDURATION:**
3–5 days

**DIMENSIONS:**
18m x 10m

**COMFORT:**
2 Plummy

**MAP REF:**
ST 745 654

**OS LANDRANGER:** 172

**PUBLIC CONVENIENCES:** Just down and to the left a bit (100 yards). It's the squat red-brick affair in the corner of the car park that's going to cause future archaeologists all manner of conundra: too big for a booth from which to collect money, too small for a car-park attendant's house – perhaps it was some sort of car-park museum exhibiting early forms of tickets and strewn with happy motorist mannequins in flat caps and plus-fours.

COMPROMISED? Try *4. The New Forest Château* (51 miles).

*'It is a truth universally acknowledged, that a single man in possession of a good fortune, must be in need of a wolf.'*

# CULTIVATING A HIDER'S MIND

Only a man careless of his reputation would refute the fact that 72 per cent of hiding is in the mind.[1] Yet scurrilously, though hiders may take endless pains over the physical aspects of concealment such as location, camouflage and costume (the Third Earl of Dunmochie habitually dressed as a 12th-century farrier when hiding from his loathsome family in the ruins of Achtenalty Castle stables in the mistaken belief that, if he were discovered, he would be assumed to be a ghost), they rarely give the inside of their brains more than a cursory glance round before embarking on the venture.

This is a grave oversight and the reason why such a large proportion of people in hiding are found sooner rather than later. A smaller proportion are found later rather than in the fullness of time, but even this must count as failure when judged against Burns's long established formula:

Success = Hiding × (Time ≥ when all the seas gang dry)

## Preparation

The key, then, is to remember that being 'in hiding' requires a completely different set of mental folk tunes to those that score the heroic struggles of your everyday life with such poignancy. Acquaint yourself with the basic melodies and at least some of the lyrics before you go, or risk the despair inherent in being reduced to a state of mind akin to that of playing air accordion while singing karaoke to a song you've never heard before and for which only every third word is coming up on the screen.

*An accordion: Frightening enough in itself, but victims claim that playing air accordion can be even more disturbing.*

[1] This rises to 76 per cent in Scotland, of course.

First, rid yourself of mental clutter. The chances are, your hiding place will be short on space so any economies of volume you can make now will pay dividends later. Since very few of the so called 'normal' mental functions are necessary when hiding, these should be discarded. The ability to communicate, for example, is entirely superfluous, though you might wish to retain a basic vocabulary if you intend to come out of hiding at some future date. Similarly, your capacity to calculate, reason and distinguish between night and day will be of negligible use to you in your new circumstances and can be expunged without a second thought (second thoughts in general can also go), although you would be advised to abandon reason last of all, just in case by doing so first you then can't work out why you were meant to jettison the other two.

Ultimately, the goal is to pare your mental faculties down to the level at which you are still able to respond to basic stimuli, but only at the third go.

### In situ
Any individual who shuns society for any length of time will, as a matter of course, be beset by demons. These are fearsome adversaries of the mental or spiritual variety, so if you find yourself physically attempting to fend them off, you can be sure that they've already won.

Demons come in many guises – loneliness ('Hello, me. May I introduce you to myself?'), self-doubt ('Oh, you've already met?'), self-pity ('And you both like each other much more than you like little old me, or rather I, that much is obvious.'). However, the most fiendish toxin is that which produces the seemingly perverse desire to be found. This is a close cousin of the criminal's repressed craving to be caught, and is well documented throughout history from the doomed flight of the Psythians all the way up to that nasty little affair in Iceland with the three-handed farmer.

### Solution
To quote the Philosopher for a moment: 'Madness is a salad in which the lettuce has been replaced by tea.' Bearing this in mind, it becomes abundantly clear that the man or woman who wishes to prevent their tomatoes from sailing like tiny red ships on a muddy sea must 'overcome their demons'. It really is as simple as that.

### Reintegration
Reassimilation into society, whether voluntary or otherwise, often comes as something of a shock. Now that you know this, it won't be, so you'll be fine.

# 9. THE OXFORD UNDERGROUNDUATE

**King's Lock, nr Wolvercote, Oxfordshire**

**NEED to KNOW:** Just a few hearty strides out of Oxford, the northernmost lock on the Thames comprises a miniature island paradise owned by the Environment Agency (and thus by you and me[1]), a wood, a weir, and a river split in twain like the plaited tresses of a sullen archduke. On this island there is a miniature paradisiacal hiding place, built by miniature hand or hands unknown, in which a subject may live like a king, albeit a stooping or diminutive one – Richard III, for example, or one of the smaller Aethelreds.

**ADVANTAGES:** Since this is an actual real bona fide hand-made hiding place with its own green PVC lining, wooden props, sandy floor, ventilation outlet and door (not shown), it needs no further work on it by the potential occupant. The roof is even covered with ivy, making it invisible to the casual observer and practically invisible to the keen one, especially if the latter is merely a keen observer of social mores or political intrigue.

**HAZARDS:** Camping is allowed on another part of the island for a small fee. Where there is camping there are, invariably, campers and this may not, of course, entirely fit in with your plans for vanishment. However, since the site is open only to those who manage to get themselves there by foot, bicycle or boat (surely everything in Britain should be run on the same principle), you will for the most part be untroubled by neighbours. Furtherhowever (if this were Germany, that word would be allowed), if you are discovered by the lock-keeper, he may see fit to charge you £5.50/night.

[1] I am assuming here that you *do* own the other half of the Environment Agency.

**LOCAL KNOWLEDGE:** The only right and proper thing to do while *in situ* here is to set about memorising Sir John Betjeman's epic autobiographical poem *Summoned by Bells*. Godstow Lock gets mentioned twice and it's just a few hundred yards along the river, you know.

**SUPPLIES:** A water tap on the west bank of the river dispenses water. If this doesn't entirely assuage your hunger, there's a sort of organic post-office affair in Wolvercote (1 mile). Don't ask them if they've got any organic stamps – they've heard that one.

**PUBLIC CONVENIENCES:** The island boasts a Spartan urinal from the minimalist school. More sophisticated water-closetorial lodgings can be found at Wolvercote.

**URBAN MYTH:** The Thames was formed by the tears of a dying seal.

**RECOMMENDED HIDURATION:**
Up to 3 weeks

**DIMENSIONS:**
2m diameter x 1m

**COMFORT:**
2 Plummy

**MAP REF:**
SP 479 104

**OS LANDRANGER:** 164

COMPROMISED? Try *16. The Roundabout* (37 miles).

*Ivy and barges – only Virgil would dare to put them in a poem together, and even he burnt the evidence afterwards.*

# 10. BAGSHOT BY BOTH SIDES

Bagshot Heath, Bagshot, Surrey

**NEED TO KNOW:** Built especially for you in the depths of this forgotten corner of Surrey, the *Bagshot by Both Sides* offers capaciousness in the grand Arcadian style without forfeiting cosiness and warmth. Created by experts to appear to consist merely of some windblown branches leaning across two fallen trees, this striking home from home goes entirely unremarked upon by casual passers-by, and even if it goes remarked, the remark is only: 'Look over there, some windblown branches leaning across two fallen trees, let's leave it well alone.' Combine this with the sleek lines of the 'Plunk' tree-trunk seat, created by a Scandinavian designer now very big in Britain though curiously unknown in his home country, to give that added touch of understated sophistication that has made you such a big hit with your friends.

**ADVANTAGES:** Instant concealment on a bed of soft pine needles. Also doubles as a hide from which to watch woodpeckers.

**HAZARDS:** It's best to keep in mind that if *Bagshot by Both Sides* is constructed upon two trees that have decided to have a bit of a lie down, the wood it inhabits might be one that is particularly susceptible to this sort of lax behaviour on the part of our arboreal cousins (lest we forget, trees and humans share 104 per cent of the same DNA). Since trees, once they decide to take the weight off their roots, just tend to flop down any old how, you might want to remain cautious without being unduly panicky, unless the creaking gets really loud.

**LOCAL KNOWLEDGE:** Although Bagshot Heath is a marvel to behold, the village itself is, essentially, a bit rubbish. Pierced through by the A30 and drained of all character it might once have had, it's really not very Surrey at all – indeed, it's a wonder that the folk at Surrey County Council haven't devised some ruse to offload it to one of their neighbours. Their counterparts at Berkshire would surely find a home for it, given that they are responsible for the most disastrous attempt at a town it is possible to imagine. But enough of Reading – in case you need to know what Bagshot is famous for, it was the scene of the 19th post-horse change (out of 21, if you're counting) taken by Lt John Richards Lapenotiere on his way from Falmouth to London to break the bitter-sweet news regarding the Battle of Trafalgar; and it has a beech tree that may have been planted by Lord Nelson but probably wasn't.

**RECOMMENDED HIDURATION:**
1–2 weeks

**DIMENSIONS:**
1m x 2m x 1.5m

**COMFORT:**
1 Plush

**MAP REF:**
SU 903 635

**OS LANDRANGER:** 175

**FREE FOOD:** The campion that grows so profusely around about is 'white' rather than 'bladder' and as such is inedible. Content yourself with a tasty pine cone and an early night.

**SUPPLIES:** The village shops (0.5 miles) are not ones to inspire and delight. There is a sort of High Street and you might possibly pick up one or two things there, but you'd be advised to bring your own. Lovers of tongue twisters will note with sadness that there is no bag shop in Bagshot.

**PUBLIC CONVENIENCES:** Bagshot's pride and joy (0.5 miles) – 24-hour service and right next to the Windle Valley Centre.

**COMPROMISED?** Try *11. The Wharf of Death* (27 miles).

*The silver birches consider their options as a pine lazes in the afternoon sun.*

# AGATHA CHRISTIE
## (1890–1976)

> **Hiduration**: 10 days
> **Value as role model**: 6/10

So, just why did Agatha Mary Clarissa Christie spend a week and a half in a Harrogate health spa posing as Mrs Teresa Neele while around the country rumours of her probable death spread like sweat on the nervous brow of a cold and calculating murderer about to be unmasked by an overweight Belgian who had seen through his alibi by deducing that the callous slaying had taken place the evening before the clocks went back and not the evening afterwards, as the police had been led to believe?

More importantly, perhaps, what lessons can the aspiring hider learn from the Duchess of Death's own unmasking by Ritchie Calder, a twenty-year-old *Daily News* crime reporter on his first assignment, a mere ten days after her disappearance?

Well, now that we are all gathered together, let us review the facts of the case in a range of irritating stock francophone accents. At 9.45pm on 3 December 1926, Mrs Christie told a member of the household staff at her Sunningdale home that she was 'going for a drive'. She left two letters – one for her secretary, Miss Fisher, leaving instructions to cancel a weekend away she was to have spent in Yorkshire, and one for her husband, Colonel Christie. Her car, a bull-nosed Morris, was discovered at 8.00 the next morning near a lake at Newlands Corner, Surrey, by fifteen-year-old 'gipsy' Jack Best. The car's bonnet was up, the lights were on, and it was covered in hoar frost. Inside lay clothes scattered from an open suitcase. Meanwhile, near his home at Giverny, Claude Monet had died.

The Surrey police reasoned correctly that the death of Monet was probably a red herring. Christie's body was obviously at the bottom of the lake and she had either committed suicide or, more probably, been murdered. Their investigations immediately centred on Colonel Christie – principally because it was reported that he was having an affair and that he and Agatha had had a blazing row on the day of her disappearance, but also because he had the sort of name you'd expect a murderer to have (they were right on this one – John Christie (no relation) was hanged in 1953 for the murder of six women). The lake was duly dragged and the Colonel secretly followed by the boys from the plain clothes division.

Meanwhile, Agatha, far from gathering slime in a watery grave, had become Teresa Neele and was following events via the newspapers (the *Daily News* was offering £100 to anyone who found her) at the Hydropathic Hotel in Harrogate, Yorkshire's poshest town (even today, if a Yorkshire person is accidentally born posh he or she is immediately herded up and sent to live there to keep the rest of the stock untainted). Everything was going just dandily: the police were searching for her hundreds of miles from where she was, and her adulterous husband was getting his comeuppance into the bargain. So, how did it all go so wrong, so quickly?

First off, she let her grim sense of humour get the better of her. Her pseudonym, Neele, was that of her husband's lover. Furthermore, she made no effort at all to change her physical appearance: she did not dress differently, dye her hair, or even bother to grow a beard. She borrowed lots of detective novels from the hotel library and openly discussed the disappearance with other guests even after they had remarked on her resemblance to photos of the missing woman. The wonder is that it took the press as long as ten days to track her down.

The official line fed to the newspapers after her rediscovery was that she had suffered some sort of short-term memory loss. However, given the sort of head for detail that Christie had, one can only conclude from this catalogue of errors that, consciously or otherwise, she actually wanted to be found.

---

**Lesson**: If you are going to disappear for a bit, do check with your subconscious mind first whether this is what it really really wants.

---

# 11. THE WHARF OF DEATH

**beneath the Oxo Tower Wharf, River Thames, London**

**NEED to KNOW:** Not unsurprisingly, the Oxo Tower Wharf was built in the late 1920s to service the Oxo Tower, home to the Liebig Extract of Meat Company. It's difficult to believe nowadays, but the company made its profits from the death of innocent animals. Let us be thankful that we live in more enlightened times. The steamer moored on the opposite bank is the HMS *President*, launched in 1918 to as much fanfare as a grieving nation could muster but now forever chained to the Victoria Embankment, a floating restaurant, venue for corporate dos, and perfect set for films based on the works of Evelyn Waugh. There's probably a moral to be winkled out there but I can't quite put my finger on it.

**ADVANTAGES:** Few people would consider it possible that you would be so quixotic as to hide somewhere that gets flushed out twice a day by hundreds of thousands of tons of water that isn't as dirty as it used to be but is still not exactly brimming with salmon. Capitalise on this, but remember to leave before the flushing begins in earnest.

**HAZARDS:** The only peril consists of occasional stray American tourists who venture bravely onto the foreshore at low tide in the wholly understandable belief that the mighty Thames is in fact the English Channel and that the exotic-looking Victoria Embankment must therefore be Franceland. Thankfully, they are liable to be too caught up in peering anxiously across the waves at the land of cheese-eating Uncle Sam-hating surrenderists to be interested in exploring beneath the wharf. Before long they'll be safely ensconced again in one of London's many US-style fast fooderies ordering freedom fries and asking where Scotland is.

**LOCAL KNOWLEDGE:** Scotland is roughly 275 miles north-north-west of here, give or take, but that's of little consequence. Assure your friendly enquirers that, for administrative reasons, it has recently been renamed 'Slough' and usher them resolutely towards Paddington station.

**FREE FOOD:** As is well known, it is against the law in the US for American citizens to stop eating. There's every chance then that something will go astray between fist and mouth during their sojourn here and that, once they've gone, you'll be able to retrieve some nutrient-free snack from the fore-shore that will last you several weeks.

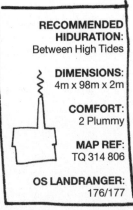

**RECOMMENDED HIDURATION:**
Between High Tides

**DIMENSIONS:**
4m x 98m x 2m

**COMFORT:**
2 Plummy

**MAP REF:**
TQ 314 806

**OS LANDRANGER:**
176/177

**SUPPLIES:** The suspiciously Franceland-sounding *Maison Brillant* at Gabriel's Wharf (0.1 miles) is not only a *patisserie* and *boulangerie* (lit. 'pattercake and boule maker') but also a *chocolatier*, which could prove dangerous. Don't be tempted by the free local delivery on offer, since this is likely to prove prejudicial to your plans for concealment.

**PUBLIC CONVENIENCES:** On the first floor of the Oxo Tower: one of the swishest loos you're likely to come across anywhere, let alone this close to a prime hiding place. One suspects they are chiefly intended for patrons of the tower's many fine art and craft boutiques but you can always have a good window shop first if you feel guilty about it.

**COMPROMISED?** Try 13. *The Pillbox-on-Crouch* (42 miles).

*St Paul's Cathedral and The Gherkin – the only two buildings in the capital that Londoners both like and can name.*

# 12. THE WOOD AT THE FOOT OF THE STAIRS

**off Dock Road, Chatham, Kent**

**NEED to KNOW:** Five steps lead down off the A231 to what a children's author of the 1950s might optimistically have called a spinney. Today the site might best be described as occupying the awkward middle colour between greenfield and brownfield. Behind what a children's author of the 1950s might have switched to calling the copse to avoid repetition is an 8-foot brick wall. What the steps might once have led to is a matter of no little speculation among the ascending/descending classes and this particular truncated flight boasts a chapter of its own in the 1950s children's classic 'My First Great Big Book of Steps That Lead to Nowhere' (Eschew the Lift Books, 1952).

**ADVANTAGES:** The brick wall snuffs out any fear of being seen from the River Medway below, while the mixed evergreen/deciduous shrubbery safeguards the hider against detection from road and pavement users.

**HAZARDS:** There is a cycle path that runs immediately past the entrance to *The Wood at the Foot of the Stairs*. Were a bicycle to choose this very point to fall apart under its rider, it is conceivable that the wretched pedal-pusher might, in his bitterness and grief, lose all sense of propriety and/or perspective and hurl the broken machine into the bushes. If you happen to be a particularly unlucky person, you might want to wear a helmet while hiding here, or at the very least take along a sign advising cyclists of the folly of pitching a bicycle into a spinney when it's probably only a gear cable that's snapped.

**LOCAL KNOWLEDGE:** Chatham may, after several glances, seem a thoroughly unpleasant place, but this is to your advantage since any would-be pursuers are unlikely to believe you capable of travelling there merely to inhabit its grim byways. Of course, if you really want to throw them off the scent – and have all hope sucked out of you at the same time – just pop next door to Gillingham (0.75 miles).

**SUPPLIES:** The High Street, Brompton (0.25 miles) boasts a capable mini-market and a couple of convenience stores, without ever really being able to discern the difference between them.

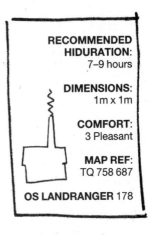

**RECOMMENDED HIDURATION:**
7–9 hours

**DIMENSIONS:**
1m x 1m

**COMFORT:**
3 Pleasant

**MAP REF:**
TQ 758 687

**OS LANDRANGER** 178

## MAKING A QUICK GETAWAY :

**BUS:** Services from Dock Road to destinations as diverse as Maidstone, Rochester and Strood.

**TRAIN:** Chatham station (0.75 miles) for all points to London, the Kent coast and Snodland.

**OTHER:** The Saxon Shore Way runs right past the entrance and takes the harassed Saxon pedestrian along the coast to Gravesend or Hastings, according to taste.

## COMPROMISED? Try 7. The Clearing (23 miles).

*Leaves – common enough nowadays but it's sobering to think that they were once paraded around Britain in travelling freak shows.*

# CONSIDERING THE VIEW

A much overlooked criterion when choosing a hiding place is the scene the prospective venue overlooks. After all, if you're going to be hiding for any length of time – shaking uncontrollably through fear, then rain and cold, then fear again as your pursuers close in, call off the search temporarily because of the rain and the cold, and then close in again – you might as well have something nice to look at.

Fortunately, when it comes to the picturesque, England, Scotland and Wales are equally blessed. Indeed, unlike some nations that have only one or two views, Britain has more than is strictly necessary. To find the right one for you, the thing to remember is that vistas are rarely unconnected with their surrounding environment. For instance, you should not expect to see a bellicose sun dipping fiercely into a violet sea while taking refuge on the outskirts of Coventry; or indeed, as Basil Fawlty so rightly pointed out, herds of wildebeest sweeping majestically across the plain from a Torquay hotel bedroom window.[1]

*Dull dull dull*

 *Ho hum*

[1] It should be noted, however, that due to the repatriation of certain panorama from countries subsumed into the Empire, it is still possible to enjoy a view of the Hindu Kush from the station platform at Mortlake.

However you settle on a prospect to your liking, do not make the schoolboy/girl error of choosing the view first and then hoping there's a nice hiding place to go with it. This is a tactic that almost always ends in tears, through which the view is bound to appear blurred and unsatisfying, thus compounding the blunder.

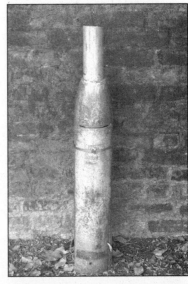

*More like it*

*Just perfect*

# 13. THE PILLBOX-ON-CROUCH

Holliwell Point, nr Burnham-on-Crouch, Essex

**NEED TO KNOW:** War, as we all know, is messy and artless (notwithstanding those fighter pilots who cut a swathe through the hearts of distaff England with their silk scarves and unfastened top buttons) so it comes as something of a bombshell to discover that the debris it leaves behind is occasionally homely and inviting. This bijou pillbox, for example, formed part of a coastal defensive line knocked up hastily in 1940. Those seeking out an authentic experience of wartime Britain will be disappointed to find that the landmines have since been removed. However, consolation comes in the view of the Holliwell Point command post (see photo opposite), a miniature hexagonal concrete castle of the Modernist school. For added historical flavour, bring along some ration books, acorn coffee and a bar of soap made out of string.

**ADVANTAGES:** Straddling the sea wall, the bunker provides excellent protection from the ravages of the North Sea. Any time that needs to be whiled away can be done so agonising over the purpose of the curious-looking pipe outlet on the seaward side.

**HAZARDS:** The River Crouch shouldn't flood, and hasn't done so for ages, but just might and, knowing your luck, will choose to do so just when you've got yourself nicely settled in with the kettle on the boil and the string worked up into an acceptable lather.

**LOCAL KNOWLEDGE:** In his *Tour Through the Whole Island of Great Britain*, Daniel Defoe contends that the average life expectancy of women who moved to Burnham on marrying was barely twelve months. This had more to do with the fog and damp than their husbands, apparently. If this were not enough, in *The War of the Worlds*, H.G. Wells has the Martians invading Britain from here. In light of these facts, it's difficult to know what to recommend in the way of precautions.

**FREE FOOD:** For reasons the locals are suspiciously secretive about, the manky remains of something that might once have been a cuttlefish appear on top of the pillbox from time to time. Best not to be around when it happens.

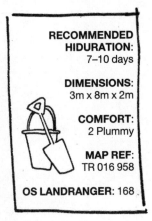

**RECOMMENDED HIDURATION:**
7–10 days

**DIMENSIONS:**
3m x 8m x 2m

**COMFORT:**
2 Plummy

**MAP REF:**
TR 016 958

**OS LANDRANGER:** 168

**SUPPLIES:** Forage for provender among the tiny shops of Burnham-on-Crouch (5 miles).

## MAKING A QUICK GETAWAY:

**BUS:** One bus every weekday to Southminster and Maldon, which isn't a lot, and none at all at weekends. Like high rollers at a Las Vegas hotel, Chelmsford and St Lawrence are better served.

**TRAIN:** Southminster at one end, Liverpool Street at the other, like so much in life.

## COMPROMISED?

Those hiding to a WWII theme should try *51. Not Angels but Angles* (266 miles).

*The medium is the message, the message in this case being: 'Please go away.'*

**Croft Castle, nr Yarpole, Herefordshire**

**NEED TO KNOW:** Granted, '00318' may not be the most evocative name for that most romantic of hiding places known to English hearts, the hollow oak tree. None of us get to choose our names: some are called Roger, others are Densil. There is no justice at birth, only whimsy. Choose to overlook the number-bearing tag piercing the imperious flank of this mighty oak, however, and you have yourself a home fit for a king-to-be fleeing the carnage of Worcester, only this wasn't the one he took cover in.

**ADVANTAGES:** You probably haven't got half the fanatical soldiery of the New Model Army looking for you so you can relax, safe from almost any likelihood of being skewered by a pike thrust from an anti-Papist.

**HAZARDS:** However, do enough research (ending triumphantly with *William's Guide to Leominster* of 1808) and you'll discover that Charles I apparently visited Croft Castle in September 1645. Your joy at discovering this and speculation as to whether the king might have got the idea for his oak-related hiding activity (see p. 132) from seeing this tree is only momentarily dampened by the realisation that you're thinking of the wrong Charles.

**ESSENTIALS:**

LOCAL KNOWLEDGE: Croft Castle was not named, as is often believed, after Colin Croft, the West Indian pace bowler, but his brother Hugh de Croft who, among other achievements, rescued Prince Edward after he had carelessly allowed himself to be kidnapped by Simon de Montfort (not the Simon de Montfort who led the Albigensian

Crusade, mind, but the one who expelled all the Jews from Leicester). Edward went on to become King Edward I and build all those rather arresting castles in Wales. This no doubt riled the few locals he hadn't managed to kill off who, with their petty short-termism and narrow historical perspective, remained obstinately blind to the benefits the castles would inevitably bring to the tourist industry just 700 years later. In truth, Hugh de Croft only happens to be the first Croft that historians have been able to put a first name to – the actual de Croft after whom the castle is named would have been a pre-Conquest Norman centuries beforehand. Oh, and in case you're still wondering, Simon de Montfort (Albigensian Crusade) was the *father* of Simon de Montfort (Jews/Leicester).

**RECOMMENDED HIDURATION:**
4–6 hours

**DIMENSIONS:**
0.8m x 0.8m x 4m

**COMFORT:**
2 Plummy

**MAP REF:**
SO 452 658

**OS LANDRANGER:**
137/148

**FREE FOOD:** The planting of a triple avenue of Spanish chestnut trees by the admirably forward-looking Herbert Croft over 350 years ago (i.e. about half the time it takes for the bad seeds of repression to produce the wild fruits of prosperity) means that the October hider need never go without chestnuts. At other times of year, you may have to mug a squirrel.

**SUPPLIES:** A co-operative shop set up and run on a voluntary basis by the splendidly counter-cultural folk of Yarpole (1 mile). Buy a cabbage: smash the system.

**PUBLIC CONVENIENCES:** Within the grounds, adjacent to the perfectly serviceable Carpenters' Shop tea room (200 yards).

**COMPROMISED?** Try *57. Holly Board* (10 miles).

*The kind of view you usually get only if you're the sort of thing that lives in a tree, like one of those frogs, only they don't live in England, so they wouldn't see this particular view, though there may be others like it in the countries where they do live.*

# HEREWARD THE WAKE
## (C. 1035–10SOMETHINGSOMETHING)

> **Hiduration**: About a year
> **Value as role model**: 4/10

Thanks to the general namby-pamby
nature of modern Britain, wholesale
slaughter is no longer viewed as an
acceptable weapon in the hider's armoury, no matter what the mitigating
circumstances. It was not ever thus, however. In the rather more robust days
of the 11th century, on those occasions when guile and cunning did not
prove a sufficient foil to ward off the unwanted attentions of one's adversaries, there was much less of a hue and cry if the hunters came to grief
courtesy of a well-judged sword thrust, the discreet administration of a red
hot poker, or the plain old-fashioned swing of a battle-axe. In those days,
being cleaved in twain was just part of growing up and not something to
whine on about, as might be the case today.

Admittedly, such practices were wont to unleash all manner of unpleasant and disproportionate retribution from the deceased's friends and
family, or (worst-case scenario) his army. This could include anything from
the torching of the hider's village to the harrying of his entire compass point
– witness William the Conqueror's 'Harrying of the North'. Indeed, said
William (rarely 'Bill', even to close friends) was really rather fond of a good
harry and would carry one out at the slightest provocation. His foray into the
north of England was of such high quality that the region was still more
or less laid waste twenty years later when the number-crunchers of the
Domesday Book visited.

It was into this bloody arena that Hereward the Wake strode one day in
1070 (he'd left England in 1062 after a bit of a contretemps with Edward the
Confessor) to take hiding to places it had never been before. More specifically, he took it to one place: the Isle of Ely in Cambridgeshire. The Isle of
Eels, as it was more poetically known back then, was an actual island
surrounded by Fenland marshes. The obvious advantage of choosing a
swamp-encircled island to hide on was that, although William the Conqueror
knew Hereward the Wake (literally 'the Wary', as you would be) was there, he
could never be sure exactly where.

Our hero's first act was to sack Peterborough Abbey, on the very proper grounds that he was saving its treasures from the dastardly Normans. William, being a dastardly Norman, thought for a bit about harrying the east but, relenting, settled for an assault on the island and the massacre of anyone found on it. Depending on whose version of events you believe, the Normans either built three wooden causeways onto the isle at Stuntney, Little Thetford and Aldreth, or one great big one, a mile long. In the latter stories, the causeway sinks beneath the weight of soldiers and horses and the Normans are chopped into little bits by Hereward and his chums. In the former, the Herewardians set fire to the bridges and chop into little bits any soldiers diving off to escape the flames. Whichever is true, it was not a red-letter day in the history of the Norman army.

Hereward could have continued thumbing his nose at the invaders almost indefinitely had he not been betrayed. Tradition has it that the monks of Ely became a bit fed up with him and told the Normans of a safe route through the marshes. Even then, His Wakeness is said to have escaped the resulting mayhem, fleeing into the Fens where he lived to skulk another day.

---

**Lesson**: The draining of land for agricultural use has left Britain bereft of inland islands. If you are planning to hide an army prior to an uprising against, say, Elizabeth II, you'd probably have to consider letting your forces mill about somewhere offshore like the Isle of Wight until they were of sufficient strength to make an assault on the mainland (on a week day, preferably, when there are more ferries).

---

# 15. THE PUMP

junction of A38(M), A5127 and A4540, Aston, Birmingham

**NEED TO KNOW:** If you must hide in Birmingham, you might as well take advantage of the city's obsession with complex road disorders. *The Pump* is situated at the fulcrum of a particularly messy one, designed to keep motorists bent on a voyage of discovery east or west from the trailblazers heading north to the question mark over humanity that is Spaghetti Junction. Engagingly, there's no indication given of what the piece of industrial frippery here pictured does or did, but it appears to have been used as some sort of pumping device at one time. Then again, maybe it still *is* some sort of pumping device and the A38(M) underpass below needs pumping or, perhaps, filling periodically. It's a Birmingham thing.

**ADVANTAGES:** If you come from a city yourself, you will blend in seamlessly with your surroundings, thus rendering you practically invisible. Hiders from rural stock should take along some city-life camouflage such as bricks, grime and as many double yellow lines as you can carry.

**HAZARDS:** It's highly probable that you could come to enjoy the location so much that you decide to settle here. Certainly the rattle and hum of several hundred vehicles trundling around you every minute is liable to mesmerise even *your* mind which tests have shown is in the top 5 per cent in the country. Death by gradual asphyxiation also a possibility.

## ESSENTIALS:

LOCAL KNOWLEDGE: Depending on whom you discuss the matter with, Villa are no match whatsoever for City or vice versa. There is no point demonstrating an opposing viewpoint by means of graphs, statistics or hard facts. If Shopping is the new Religion, then Football is the new Politics.

**FREE FOOD**: If anything edible grew here, it would provide a meal fit only for toxicologists. Better to fast. If you do this for long enough, the cars begin to take on the form of immense snails, a phenomenon that at least helps to pass the time.

**SUPPLIES**: Stagger, hungry beyond hunger itself, westward to the shining food palaces of Newtown, northward to central Aston or eastward to Vauxhall. Try to avoid the snails.

**PUBLIC CONVENIENCES**: Thankfully, you won't be needing any.

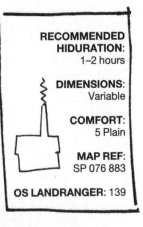

**RECOMMENDED HIDURATION**:
1–2 hours

**DIMENSIONS**:
Variable

**COMFORT**:
5 Plain

**MAP REF**:
SP 076 883

**OS LANDRANGER**: 139

### MAKING A QUICK GETAWAY:

**BUS**: Catch one of the very biggest snails from here to all parts of Birmingham and none.

**TRAIN**: Duddeston station (0.75 miles) for Lichfield and its enticing Lily Pond, and Redditch which does without.

**BARGE**: The Birmingham and Fazeley Canal and the Grand Union Canal are both within a couple of hundred yards. The latter will take you all the way to London, a mere 166 locks away, while the former leads to Fazeley, whatever that is.

### COMPROMISED? Try *22. The Lily Pond* (14 miles).

*Birmingham, twinned with Elysium.*

# 16. THE ROUNDABOUT

**Europa Way, nr Heathcote, Warwickshire**

**NEED TO KNOW:** Is it hubris or a sign of some greater malaise at the heart of England that the meeting of the A452 with three minnowy lanes should merit such a profoundly grandiose roundabout? Built just a few short years ago by air-lifting in an entire Hebridean island and knocking off the sharp bits, the roundabout is less a road feature than a socio-historical event. This is truly the 'Lennon bumps into McCartney in a car park' of the tarmacadamed world. It also sports a rather nice bit of lawn – presumably sown after the rocky doughnut had been ripped from the Atlantic waves, since there's not a sheep dropping on it – which girds the would-be spinney like a protective green moat, albeit a somewhat ineffectual one.

**ADVANTAGES:** No one in their or anyone else's right mind is likely to think of looking for a person in a roundabout so your chances of being discovered here are slim to analgesic. Furthermore, the vegetation – a sort of Council Standard No. 3 Pack (Shrubs and Trees) mixed with local windborne varieties – is dense enough to keep any occupants from the view of the circling masses in both summer and winter.

**HAZARDS:** As is well known, a noisy noise annoys an oyster and it's no coincidence that oysters have given this roundabout a wide berth. Singing very loudly in order to block out the aural onslaught is inadvisable since at some point someone will work out that even the most tutored of wildlife is unlikely to know *all* the words to 'The Girl From Ipanema'.

## ESSENTIALS:

**FREE FOOD:** Elderberries, rosehips. Teasels, while inedible, are handy for scooping honey or any similar semi-viscous fluid out of jars. Do check what the similar semi-viscous fluids are though, before eating.

**SUPPLIES:** Spoilt for choice what with Warwick and Leamington Spa both being just a mile away. However, Warwick trumps its neighbour with Harlequin, a costume-hire shop in Smith Street (see **How to be Disguised**, p. 148).

**READING MATTER:** Aleksandr Solzhenitsyn's *The First Circle*. Dive into the happy happy world of Gleb Nerzhin, the brilliant mathematician watching his life drain away in the Mavrino Sharashka prison while he aids and abets the state security apparatus that put him there.

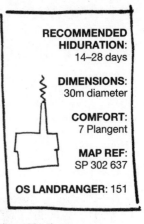

**RECOMMENDED HIDURATION:**
14–28 days

**DIMENSIONS:**
30m diameter

**COMFORT:**
7 Plangent

**MAP REF:**
SP 302 637

**OS LANDRANGER:** 151

## MAKING A QUICK GETAWAY:

**BUS:** Once an hour, the 75 will take you to Budbrooke, a medieval village whose sole remains are a moat, a fishpond and a bus service – a pleasant departure from the *Sturm und Drang* of roundabout life.

**TRAIN:** Warwick or Leamington Spa for London, Birmingham and, for the iambic pentameterally inclined, Stratford-upon-Avon.

## COMPROMISED? Try *15. The Pump* (20 miles).

*Roundabouts were introduced in Britain in the mid-1960s as a metaphor for something or other but were opened up to traffic soon afterwards.*

# THE ART OF CAMOUFLAGE

Mention the word 'camouflage' to most people and they'll immediately think of those awkward netting arrangements slung over tanks in 1950s films starring an ensemble of British character actors desperately attempting to look battle-hardened and rugged like they did during their own war service which, admittedly, consisted entirely of ENSA concerts for troops stationed in Bangalore.

Unfortunately, besides the fact that the Army tends to get a bit peevish if you attempt to borrow its camouflage netting (even just for weekends), it's really of no value at all to the average hider (i.e. one that doesn't resemble an armoured vehicle). If you're not convinced, try throwing one over yourself and walking down the High Street. Invisible you're not.

The secret of good camouflage is its adaptability to its surroundings and the thing it's meant to be camouflaging. In a suburban environment, for example, there's no point in dressing up as a cow since this is only likely to draw attention to yourself (see High Street camouflage netting experience, above). Nor should you be lured towards the other extreme and attempt to disguise yourself as, say, a cul-de-sac. However lifelike the cul-de-sac may be, and however well it fits into the suburban setting, there will always be some busybody with an A–Z who queries whether it should be there at all and ends up phoning the police.

The key word here is 'appropriate'. If you're in a tree, by all means cover yourself in leaves. However, if you're floating in the sea and wish to make

*The fifteen members of the Army's crack self-camouflage unit demonstrate the effectiveness of their now-famous special issue 'all-over grass outfits'.*

yourself less noticeable, the leaves trick is going to be of very little practical value unless a nearby ship has just shed a cargo of fresh foliage after listing badly in heavy seas.

To cut to the chase, there are three basic forms of camouflage that every hider should master.

### In town

Urban areas are grey places filled with grey people who have never seen the sea and believe that milk is the juice of some kind of fruit that is grown in a hot country. Unlike the countryside, towns and cities are full of mess, debris and fragments of things. This makes camouflage exceptionally easy. For example, one very effective urban disguise – particularly on building sites or wasteland – is to throw a grey sheet over yourself and remain absolutely still. If you also assume a sort of sprawling pose, you will be taken for some undefined mess or debris. Advanced hiders can even make themselves appear to be fragments of things.

### In the countryside

Although it is true to say that most things in the countryside (road kill excepted) are green or brown and shades in between, it is a mistake to think that these are the only colours you need employ when merging with a rustic backdrop. For example, one very effective rural disguise – particularly on windswept moorland or blasted heath – is to throw a grey sheet over yourself and remain absolutely still. From a distance you will be taken for a standing stone. If you find yourself in a place unlikely to have been chosen for its spiritual or astronomical significance by our ancestors, simply take the same course of action and pose as a trig. point.

### At sea

So often, would-be camoufleurs make the mistake of thinking that the sea is blue. Since the sea reflects the sky, the colour of the water is determined by the state of the heavens above it and, as we all know, the weather is always a bit dodgy out to sea. This is why it is rarely the blue of our imaginings but rather a dull grey. Happily, this helps to facilitate one's efforts to melt into the seascape. For example, one very effective marine disguise – particularly in fast-flowing channels or coastal inlets – is to throw a grey sheet over yourself and remain absolutely still. From a distance, you will be taken for water. Given time and practice, you may even be taken for salt water, though most experts agree that this is seldom worth the trouble expended on it.

# 17. THE HUT

River Cam, Sheeps Green, Cambridge

**NEED TO KNOW:** You know you're on a posh river when it's got two names and the one the locals favour is the Latin one (see also *9. The Oxford Undergroundduate*). Hence this dainty residence might well be on the Cam to you and me, but is most certainly on the Granta to the natives. Anyway, there's a fine abandoned hut here with an ornate inward-swinging gate (not shown). Don't be put off by the fact that it looks like the sort of place that, if you were of a certain age, or a certain under-age, you might appropriate for an illicit cigarette.

**ADVANTAGES:** Cambridge is, of course, a terribly intellectual place full of people who know arcane things about science such as what you would get if $\gamma\mu\delta^2$ were pelted with super-negative neutrons for two microns of a second and then left to cool for a bit. Most of these kind gentle people, however, have difficulty in tying their own shoes, so the chances of any of them being able to track down even the most careless of hiders are slim indeed.

**HAZARDS:** The appearance, in and out of season, of bridge jumpers. These are folk of both sexes who dress in wet suits and baggy things and jump off bridges. Almost always, they hit the river. Once they have done so, they swim over to the bank as best they can in a baggy sort of way and, if their lust for thrills is still not sated, jump off the bridge again. These champions of the experiential shouldn't trouble you too much since they are too wrapped up in their pastime to notice anyone or anything else, but it's best to be forewarned. In times of loneliness the rhythmic 'squeeeee – thok' of their bridge jumping can actually be quite comforting.

**ESSENTIALS:**

**LOCAL KNOWLEDGE:** The folly adjacent to *The Hut* (see below) sports the famous lower-case motto: 'fait bien' ('do well'). It goes without saying that this is the shortened form of the famous French lower-case maxim meaning: '(you'd) do well (not to hide here, for it hath not much in the way of walls).' Good advice it is too.

**FREE FOOD:** There's some hawthorn around, which always makes for a satisfying jelly come the autumn.

**SUPPLIES:** The Co-operative store on Grant-chester Street (0.5 miles) stocks most things, many of them fairly traded. You can also become a member of the co-operative and go to annual general meetings and stuff. It's all rather exciting.

**PUBLIC CONVENIENCES:** Over the bridge and straight on (100 yards).

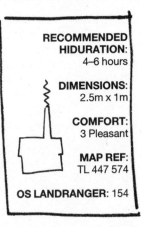

**RECOMMENDED HIDURATION:**
4–6 hours

**DIMENSIONS:**
2.5m x 1m

**COMFORT:**
3 Pleasant

**MAP REF:**
TL 447 574

**OS LANDRANGER:** 154

MAKING A QUICK GETAWAY:

**OTHER:** A vertical journey off the bridge tends to start with promising speed but then gets bogged down after the first six feet or so. A more fruitful exit might be had by means of some sort of river-going vessel. A rowing boat or canoe will, with a bit of effort on your part, take you out onto the Fens one way, or to Great Shelford and points south-east the other.

COMPROMISED? Try 24. *Revenge of the Fifty-Foot Herring* (43 miles).

*'fait bien (et ne te cache pas ici, parce qu'il y a très peu si on parle de murs)'*

# 18. THE THETFORD CRATER

Croxton Heath, nr Thetford, Norfolk

**NEED TO KNOW:** About half a mile to the north is a crater called The Devil's Punchbowl. There's a picnic area there and everything (well, all right, just a picnic area). The crater is so called because the Devil actually once used it as a punchbowl. This might seem a foolish thing to do since a) it's full of grass and plants and trees and things, and b) the ground is porous. Neither of these qualities will you find cropping up anywhere in Good Punch guides, even those that tie in to cheaply made television programmes. What then might this more southerly crater be? After all, the Devil is hardly likely to make the same elementary mistake twice. The possibilities range from the natural (it's a natural crater, formed by the peculiar but purely natural order of natural things) to the man-made (it's the result of a bomb dropped by some Heinkel gone astray) to the supernatural (it was dug by gangs of slave pixies on the orders of the occasionally evil but largely misunderstood High Lord Asam of the Troglodytes). In the final analysis, what matters most is that it has very steep sides and a depth of about 20m, and getting out is considerably harder than getting in.

**ADVANTAGES:** Imagine you owned a wood that had a cellar in it and that that cellar was itself a wood. The advantages are obvious.

**HAZARDS:** The major hazard is that the crater is itself hazardous. Extreme caution should be taken because a broken ankle here would do neither you nor your ankle any good.

**ESSENTIALS:**

LOCAL KNOWLEDGE: *The Thetford Crater* should not be confused with the 112-mile-wide Chicxulub Crater in the Yucatán, the alleged point of impact of a meteorite that caused such colossal climate change on Earth that it is thought to have wiped out the dinosaurs. Whatever the cause of the Thetford Crater, no dinosaurs are likely to have been injured. The worst that might have happened was that one or two were mildly put out. A brontosaurus, for instance, might have discovered that he had to go around the crater in order to get to a water hole. Something of that order.

**FREE FOOD:** Pine cones (edible raw but even tastier toasted), beech nuts (ditto) and bracken (the curled fronds only – treat as you would asparagus).

**SUPPLIES:** The village store in Croxton (1 mile) contains all that you might imagine but slightly less, if you find they've run out of certain products you'd imagined or they simply don't stock them because there's no demand locally.

**PUBLIC CONVENIENCES:** Not really.

**RECOMMENDED HIDURATION:**
2–4 days

**DIMENSIONS:**
50m diameter

**COMFORT:**
4 Placid

**MAP REF:**
TL 878 883

**OS LANDRANGER:** 144

## MAKING A Quick GETAWAY:

**TRAIN:** Not every station can boast a direct service to both Nottingham and Cambridge with occasional forays to Liverpool and London. But then not every station is Thetford station (3 miles) which, on second thoughts, is probably just as well or the railway system would be plunged into chaos (all right then, further chaos).

## COMPROMISED?

Try *17. The Hut* (32 miles).

*On long summer evenings, the mournful laments of slave pixies emanate from these woods even today.*

# 19. ORFORD NEST

The Gull, Gedgrave Marshes, nr Orford, Suffolk

**NEED TO KNOW:** Well, well, what do we have here? Some sort of corn-circle affair by the looks of it, except that the corn is long grass, the circle is an oval and the alien spacecraft responsible must have come all the way from the planet Twee, because this one's no more than about a metre in diameter. It does make you wonder just how advanced these other civilisations are – they come millions of light years just to see us and then end up mucking about in a field before promptly leaving again. I bet they're half-way home when they dash their eight hands against their eight foreheads and exclaim: 'Nggg, hfhfyt yapppppig gwtwtiiiiii. Encrrrunfwa.' ('Bother, we forgot to say hello. Again.')

**ADVANTAGES:** Thank goodness the folk from Twee are the 'OO'-scale titans of the universe because the fruit of their labours, *Orford Nest* (not to be confused with the nearby Orford Ness), is just right for one person, or four reasonably compact spaniels, to curl up inside. Simply remove spaniels and make yourself cosy. The longer grass surrounding the nest protects you from all and sundry, whether by land or by water. Indeed, if global warming makes sea mist a permanent feature of the Suffolk coast, as I idly speculate it might, you will be able to hide here more or less indefinitely.

**HAZARDS:** Orford Ness sounds a bit like Awful Mess. Don't get yourself into one of these because, like A Bit of a Jam or A Terrific Fix, they can be tricky to get out of and before you do so you'll find yourself talking like some character out of a P.G. Wodehouse novel and that's not going to help.

**LOCAL KNOWLEDGE:** Most of the Ness was appropriated by the War Office in 1913 and used for various mysterious warlike experiments. This was followed up in the 1950s (what a curious old decade *that* was) by the construction of some pagodas. Apparently these were used, not for pagoding, as one might imagine, but for the testing of atomic bombs, though without their atomic bits. So they say.

**FREE FOOD:** The water of The Gull, that being the strip of river just in front of you, should be fresh enough but then it is jolly close to the sea so you might want to try some out in a cup of tea first. If the tea tastes salty, that's probably the water, and you should discard it responsibly.

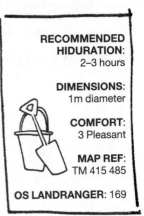

**RECOMMENDED HIDURATION:**
2–3 hours

**DIMENSIONS:**
1m diameter

**COMFORT:**
3 Pleasant

**MAP REF:**
TM 415 485

**OS LANDRANGER:** 169

**SUPPLIES:** Orford (1 mile) is a funny little village but I think you'll like it. It's all terribly coastal without actually being on the coast, there being a river and a lump of Ness in between it and the foaming brine.

**PUBLIC CONVENIENCES:** Really quite acceptable ones can be found in Baker's Lane, Orford (1.2 miles).

**COMPROMISED?** Try *13. The Pillbox-on-Crouch* (44 miles).

*The Orford Ness monster makes a rare appearance.*

63

# HOW TO CROUCH

It is a truth universally acknowledged that the smaller you are, the easier it is to hide.

Imagine yourself, if you will, sitting on a comfortable sofa in your drawing-room dipping into the latest Daphne du Maurier while wood pigeons coo themselves into silence in the bleak October dawn beyond the French windows. Submerged in a world of heather-blown heroines and courtly Cornish coves, are you likely to notice the arrival of, say, a dormouse? Compare and contrast your lack of reaction to *Muscardinus avellanarius* with that engendered by the entrance of, say, a whale. The most sumptuous of armchairs will struggle to mask completely the presence of even the smaller sort
of cetacean mammal. Looking up from the slightly over-written passage in chapter four, you enquire of the creature as to its business, curtly request that in future it makes an appointment before calling, and show it to the door. In the meantime, the dormouse remains unnoticed among the kindling in the fireplace, happy and smug in equal measure until it is accidentally thrown into the fire by Havill, the under-butler whose flaxen moustache has quickened the heart of more than one impressionable young scullery maid.

Let us learn from the animals, then, and make ourselves small. Liposuction might help in this regard, of course, but is by no means for everyone. A less drastic means of self-miniaturisation is the simple crouch. Crouching has saved lives in the past and yet is shamefully overlooked in a society where Complexity has become synonymous with Progress, and in which Evolution has become Convolution.

For those readers unfamiliar with the art of random capitalisation as a sign of mock scholarliness, there follows this step-by-step guide to the rudiments.

## The Non-Crouch

Before you know how to crouch, it is best to know what a crouch is not. Here, Evelyn is non-crouching behind a wall. His friend Bethany has spotted him easily and is pointing longingly at his bag of sherbet lemons.

### The High Crouch

Evelyn has adopted the high crouch position behind the wall. His friend Jocelyn is fairly certain that Bethany told her that Evelyn was behind the wall with a bag of sherbet lemons but now she cannot be sure.

### The Low Crouch

Denholm has found a bush. He adopts a low crouch behind it and is entirely hidden from view. Densil can see the bush but now believes his twin may have moved to Canada as threatened in his last letter.

### The Crab Crouch

Cecil is seen here crab crouching behind a medium-sized compost bin, the only cover for 400 miles in the vast salt plains of Utah. The resultant build up of lactic acid in his biceps is offset by the knowledge that only those employing the services of spotter planes

or spy satellites will be able to track him down. As the pain in his upper arms increases, he imagines what it would be like if someone cared enough to do so.

## 20. REEDY BED

nr Berney Arms, just a bit west of Breydon Water, Norfolk

**NEED to KNOW:** Norfolk is the Scotland of England. Nowhere in the nation formerly known as Albion can one feel quite so remote as in East Anglia's much ridiculed northern third. Sadly, it is also true that in few counties can there be said to be less to hide behind. This means that a little cunning is called for. In actual fact, a very little cunning indeed will usually suffice since at 1.52 people per hectare, Norfolk is one of the lesser populated counties in England and so your chances of being detected are at the happier end of the rainbow, probably somewhere around orange.

**ADVANTAGES:** True socialism is based on the equality of manners, as E.M. Forster helpfully pointed out, presumably without canvassing too many poor people on the matter first. The joy of *Reedy Bed* is that, like death and true socialism, it is a great leveller, for here both prince and pauper must lie down if they are to take advantage of its shallow grassy walls. There's really only room for one incumbent at a time, however, and I can't imagine the prince – even one with no realistic hope of becoming king such as Prince Edward – standing around while the pauper hides snugly in the reeds below. So much for meritocracy.

**HAZARDS:** Friends cannot travel through the post, as E.M. Forster helpfully pointed out, presumably having requested his chums to try out the theory first. Therefore, you should not hold out any hope that one might be delivered here to help you when your arm is inevitably broken by one of the many local swans.

**LOCAL KNOWLEDGE:** The phrase 'NfN' should probably not be used within the borders of Norfolk since it refers to practices that might be deemed eccentric in the rest of the country but which are 'Normal for Norfolk'. In case you let it slip accidentally and are challenged about it by locals, ask them to explain the all-too-frequent instances in fields around the county of maniacally grinning robots fashioned out of hay bales, hub caps and sundry tractor parts. In the end, perhaps it's wise to remember that, as the poet says: 'There is no such thing in life as normal.'

**FREE FOOD:** Reeds. Avoid the cowbane if you can, for a single mouthful will kill you. Unless, of course, it's cow parsley.

**RECOMMENDED HIDURATION:**
7–10 days

**DIMENSIONS:**
2m x 0.5m

**COMFORT:**
2 Plummy

**MAP REF:**
TG 452 059

**OS LANDRANGER:** 134

**SUPPLIES:** Your best bet is to trek across to the Berney Arms (1.2 miles), one of a select band of pubs in Britain that cannot be accessed by road – indeed, unless you come by rail, river or from *Reedy Bed*, you might as well stay indoors and enjoy a good evening's whimpering.

**PUBLIC CONVENIENCES:** Ah, right, yes, well. Great Yarmouth, probably (4.5 miles).

**TRAIN:** Berney Arms (0.7 miles) is apparently Britain's smallest station and one of a select band that cannot be accessed by road – indeed, unless you come by rail, etc. etc.

Try *18. The Thetford Crater* (36 miles).

*Norfolk – according to official government records, there's nothing here.*

# 21. RAILWAY STAIRS

'twixt the River Severn and the railway station, Shrewsbury, Shropshire

**NEED to KNOW:** Accessible from a pleasingly informal entrance half-way down the steps that take the unwary pedestrian from Victoria Street to the River Severn, the hangman's noose around the guilty neck of Shropshire's only county town.

**ADVANTAGES:** The perfect place to lie up and wait until the heat's off if you've just escaped from HM Prison Shrewsbury – less than a minute away, even to those encumbered by shackles, balls, chains, thumb-screws and any of the other filigree-ree of penal life. If you're one of those inmates who can't get enough of sycamore trees or those nameless plants one only ever sees in the lee of railway lines you might want to consider bringing a sleeping bag and making a summer of it.

**HAZARDS:** Just the other side of the wall is Shrewsbury station so it's not one of your more tranquil spots unless your sojourn here coincides with a strike or a day in which the wrong sort of air is causing the trains to slow down sufficiently for there to be no point in making them go at all.

## ESSENTIALS:

**LOCAL KNOWLEDGE:** As is well known, Shrewsbury derives its name from the ancient practice of burying shrews. This is a tradition kept alive in the town every 24 years in the August Ceremony of the Burial of the Shrew in which a plastic shrew, hand chiselled by local craftsmen, is buried up to its waist in the beard of the town's chief privy councillor. The ritual can sometimes take up to eight weeks to perform so it's wise to book some time off work. Next ceremony 2012.

**SUPPLIES:** That which Shrewsbury cannot supply, the heart desireth not. See also, its very own sort of dull biscuit.

**PUBLIC CONVENIENCES:** A grimly industrial construct at the bus station (0.25 miles) – the sort where a sheet of irregularly polished metal serves as a mirror.

**URBAN MYTH:** It is believed by many that Charles Darwin, who was born and schooled in Shrewsbury, was the founder of Marxism. This is not so.

**READING MATTER:** The only proper literature to read in these parts is *Das Kapital* by Charles Darwin or 'The Dread of Falling into Naught' by local hero Wilfred Owen (although of course it was his brother, Harold, who was born here – food for thought as cold agues in your hectic limbs convulse).

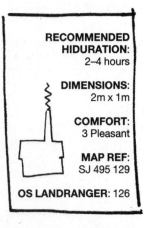

**RECOMMENDED HIDURATION:**
2–4 hours

**DIMENSIONS:**
2m x 1m

**COMFORT:**
3 Pleasant

**MAP REF:**
SJ 495 129

**OS LANDRANGER:** 126

MAKING A QUICK GETAWAY:

**BUS:** Bus stationeers can find themselves wafted to Oswestry (where Harold Owen's brother was born), Montgomery or Ludlow.

**TRAIN:** Train stationeers (20 yards as the leaf clusters) can find themselves wafted to Bristol, Prees, Pwllheli or Machynlleth if they're not careful.

COMPROMISED? Try 59. *The Trough* (19 miles).

*Three travellers, laden with souvenir shrews, miss their train which has tip-toed in on the platform behind them 'just for a laugh'.*

# HIDING AT HOME

In the same way that a lot of people in this country pooh-pooh Australian table decorations, so huge swathes of the population dismiss out of hand the concept of hiding at home. 'It cannot be and it *must* not be done', trumpet retired colonels from East Sheen; 'Hiding – it's, like, for the outdoors, man', argue hippies clinging to driftwood in the Irish Sea; 'I tried hiding at home once but the freezer door jammed and I froze to death', say mediums pretending to have conjured the spirits of the recent hapless dead.

All of these people are, of course, wrong and, in an ideal world, their defeatism and lack of imagination would be made illegal, replacing on the statute books so-called criminal offences such as leering or causing others to leer at a privy councillor's knees (the 'Genusmirk' Bill of 1910 that nearly did for Asquith); membership of the Ancient Order of Perambulists (1692); and the pitch-forking of truculent youths (legal precedent – Giles vs Crudworthless, 1952).

Just sit and stare at the advantages for a while.

## The advantages

Not only is the home dazzlingly cornucopic in the depth and variety of its hiding places, it is unarguably convenient, it being on your doorstep, so to speak. You can also break cover for a minute or two to make a cup of tea if the coast is clear. Furthermore, if you really don't want to be found, you can lock all the doors and keep everyone out.

Stack this hefty bunch up against the fly-weight from the land of the Glass Half Empty and just see what transpires.

## The disadvantages

As far as can be ascertained there is only one disadvantage to domicile concealment. If you are hiding from agents of the law, locking yourself in will do no good since this merely gives them the occasion to kick your front door in, shouting, 'Police! Police!' – an event your everyday copper lives for. They buy special shoes for the purpose and cut a notch in the heel for each door broken down. Next time you pass a policeman, ask him to show you the notches in his heel – he will not deny you. If he is from the Guardia Civil, it is customary to exclaim, '¡Buenas Notches!' and flee for your life.

The ayes have it, I think.

## Around the home

A number of rooms in the home lend themselves particularly to the business of temporary disappearance.

### *The kitchen*

All kitchens are liberally festooned with cupboards, many of which are not opened from one year's end to the next on account of the fact that they contain nothing but the eccentric bric-a-brac of a faddish age – soda siphons, fajita dishes, egg-slicers and espresso machines are just a few of the *must have will have* devices lurking there waiting to ensnare archaeologists from the future (see also *8. Royal Crescent Garden*). Simply cart these off to your charity shop of choice and fill, with your person, the space thus vacated. Lie back[1] and enjoy the catharsis.

**NB** Do not attempt to secrete yourself inside ovens (including so-called 'microwave' ovens), dishwashers or liquidisers except *in extremis*.

---

[1] Degree of recumbency will depend on size of cupboard – consult your stockist for details.

*The study/library*
Some posh types (and *soi-disant* posh types with a box room they've no other use for) have what they refer to as *a study*. For appearances' sake, if nothing else, this will have been furnished with a bookcase, though the books in it might sometimes be replicas. Edge this bookcase forward from the wall and creep in behind it. Take a book (or replica) with you to amuse yourself (or replicate the sensation of amusement) while hidden.

Really posh types have a room they off-handedly call *the library*, despite the visions of blood on the Persian carpet and a murdered earl slumped over the desk with a knife protruding from his back that this will inevitably bring to mind. Libraries are, of course, strewn with bookcases. One of these will be false and act as secret door to a mysterious room beyond containing a locked portmanteau. The door is activated by a lever hidden among his lordship's collection of antique billiard cues. No, not that one, the second one down. There you go. Surprisingly smooth action for its age. Apparently Anne Boleyn hid here during the Peasants' Revolt etc. etc.

*The attic/cellar*
If you are blessed with *an attic* or *a cellar* (if you are not sure, go home and try ascending or descending further than you would normally – if you cannot, you aren't; if, on the other hand, you are pleasantly surprised to find you are able to go down further but find it cramped, you are in a drain), you will find either admirably suited to the needs of the domestic hider. Not only are they roomier than run-of-the-mill home-produced hiding places such as wardrobes and tumble dryers, they can often support human life for long periods of time – in the case of attics by the fortuitous provision of a water tank, and in cellars by a stock of pre-Napoleonic champagnes.[2]

[2] Note that some cellars may be limited to champagnes from 1800 onwards.

## Hiding at home

*Not to be confused with hiding in the Home Counties.*

### Warning

On no account hide under a bed. Aside from being an activity more appropriate to children, you will find that, if you are unearthed, journalists will invariably report that you were discovered *cowering* under a bed, as if there were no other attitude a person could adopt beneath a double divan. Indeed, being a careless lot, they are more than likely to state that you were discovered cowering under your own bed (regardless of whether you had crawled under the twins' bunks or the baby's cot), thus exacerbating the humiliation.

Also, the dust fairies don't like it.

# 22. THE LILY POND

**Beacon Park, Lichfield, Staffordshire**

**NEED to KNOW:** You'll want to bring a straw with you for this one or you may find the environment somewhat constricting. A plain straw is best since anything too colourful could draw the attention of the park-keeper. Keeping the upper end of the straw above the surface of the water at all times, lie down on your back in the pond and ease yourself under the crust of vegetation we shall, for the sake of brevity, call lily pads. Try to imagine that you are the *Titanic* and that you have injudiciously chosen to ram an iceberg. To help you get into role, look up at the blurry form outlined against the malignant wintry sky. This bronze statue, just a few feet from your supine body, is a representation of none other than Commander Edward John Smith, the captain of the ill-fated liner. Unlike him, you can rise from your watery bed. Rejoice that it is so.

**ADVANTAGES:** Assuming you stay still and keep breathing, you are unlikely to be disturbed by anyone at all, thus making the spot one of the best short-term hiding places in all of south Staffordshire.

**HAZARDS:** Death by drowning. Bronchial pneumonia. Fish.

**ESSENTIALS:**

**LOCAL KNOWLEDGE:** The writer, wit and lexicographer Dr Samuel Johnson was born at the nearby Samuel Johnson Birthplace Museum in what was then a network of little streets. In case that's unclear, his dictionary's definition of 'network' was 'any thing reticulated, or decussated, at equal distances, with interstices between the intersections'.

**FREE FOOD:** Bread, possibly, if someone mistakes your shadowy form for a large grebe.

**SUPPLIES:** Lichfield's Quonians Lane boasts a retailer of ecclesiastical masonry which could probably rustle you up a very fetching headstone if you accidentally fall asleep *in situ*.

**PUBLIC CONVENIENCES:** Clean-up operations can be effected a stone's throw away at Beacon Park's own facilities situated on the corner of Swan Road and Beacon Street.

**IF IT ALL GETS TOO MUCH:** The cathedral, but a mere hymnal's hurl away, is lovely, albeit that the bowl of the font is unsuitable as a place of concealment, filled or unfilled.

**RECOMMENDED HIDURATION:**
30–35 minutes

**DIMENSIONS:**
4m x 3m x 0.5m (deep)

**COMFORT:**
9 Playful

**MAP REF:**
SK 095 114

**OS LANDRANGER:** 128

MAKING A QUICK GETAWAY:

**BUS:** There are horribly frequent services to many enthralling Midlands destinations including Birmingham, Sutton Coldfield, Stafford and Tamworth.

**TRAIN:** Lichfield City station (0.6 miles) is your one-stop shop for journeys to Brum and all stations to Redditch.

**OTHER:** For shorter journeys, try backstroke.

COMPROMISED? Try *15. The Pump* (14 miles). If you've just come from *The Pump*, it may be time to give yourself up.

*Captain Smith, rumoured to have been demonstrating this very Russian dancing technique when disaster struck.*

# 23. THE QUATREFOIL TOWER

off Lower Church Street, Ashby de la Zouch, Leicestershire

**NEED TO KNOW:** Stinging nettles girdle an isolated brick tower. The Royalist stronghold at Ashby de la Zouch was captured by the Round-heads in 1646 and slighted two years later, which explains the look of utter dismay still registering on the face of the castle today.

**ADVANTAGES:** The tower effectively shields the hider from the gaze of visitors to the castle itself. Two sycamore trees very nearly give shelter from the vicissitudes of the sky – expect some decent protection from the attentions of spy satellites in about ten years' time.

**HAZARDS:** When someone last took the trouble to count them (1997), there were 13,068 people in Ashby de la Zouch. It is conceivable that, during any given half hour, one of them might take it into his or her head to stroll down the path leading from Lower Church Street to the playing field, thus passing the tower. At night this is not a problem since you can disappear into the shadows. However, by day you should do your best to melt into your surroundings by dressing in green and stinging anyone who inadvertently brushes past you.

## ESSENTIALS:

**LOCAL KNOWLEDGE:** Ashby de la Zouch was the setting for large chunks of *Ivanhoe*, Sir Walter Scott's novel of love, death and excessive courtesy in the days when Doncaster could still be described without irony as a 'pleasant town'.

**FREE FOOD:** Nettle soup (see **Plant Life and How to Eat It**, p. 106) is not only highly nutritious and as tasty a meal as any the length and breadth of England, but is efficacious in the treatment of gout, apparently.

**SUPPLIES:** The town is chock-full of retailers eager to meet all your seclusionist needs.

**PUBLIC CONVENIENCES:** Kilwardby Street (0.3 miles). A fee of 10 pence is charged – a sure sign of ill-breeding.

**READING MATTER:** If the limpid gaze of ennui alights on you while you loiter here, try committing to memory the glossary at the back of *Ivanhoe*. The 240 words and phrases therein are serviceable in a variety of social settings. *Clerk me no clerks* ('Kindly address me not as a priest'), for example, might come in very handy when dealing with psychotic medievalists who erroneously assume that because you are mumbling in a sort of Normanised Latin you must be conducting their marriage service – an all too common occurrence on public transport nowadays.

**RECOMMENDED HIDURATION:**
30–35 minutes

**DIMENSIONS:**
1m x 0.75m

**COMFORT:**
6 Plebeian

**MAP REF:**
SK 362 165

**OS LANDRANGER:** 128

## MAKING A QUICK GETAWAY:

**BUS:** Hourly services waft the discerning passenger to Burton upon Trent, Nuneaton, Leicester, Heather and Newtown Burgoland. However, a change at Ibstock is in order for those wishing to visit Newtown Unthank, Leicestershire's unlikeliest village, though they'd unthank you for saying so.

## COMPROMISED? Try 29. *The M1* (19 miles).

*Mary, Queen of Scots, slept here and was subsequently executed. Bring stimulants.*

# PHOBIAS

Motivational speakers may claim that you have 'nothing to fear but fear itself' – a message that goes down only too well with a phobophobic audience – but analyse the statement for a moment and it's less helpful than they would have you believe. After all, fear is quite frightening – otherwise, what would be the point of it?

Indeed, if you feel you must have an excuse to go into hiding, fear would seem to be right up there with the greats.[1] The trouble comes when you arrive at your chosen spot only to find the fear waiting for you, looking relaxed and stubbing imaginary cigarette butts into the ground. Unfortunately, there's not much to be done about this except, perhaps, wonder at why fear keeps up such a pretence of smoking. The only course of action to take in such circumstances is to scream until you pass out.

Now, I imagine your own fears are perfectly rational ones and nothing at all to be ashamed about. However, just in case there's a chance they might be a teensy-weensy bit irrational, here are three common phobias against which you may measure your own, so at least you have the pleasure of knowing what you're screaming about before you slip into unconsciousness.

**Dextrophobia** *A fear of objects to the right of the body*[2]
In tests, eight out of ten hiders were unearthed by somebody approaching from the right, so those naturally gifted in the art of concealment will probably discover that dextrophobia has long since been part of their make-up. This fear can be allayed only by moving to the far edge of the Universe and turning 90° anti-clockwise, leaving the sufferer with literally nothing to fear. If such a remedy is inconvenient for any reason, try choosing a hiding place where whatever is to your right is something of which you might be reasonably fearful: an erupting volcano, say, or an incurable disease. With any luck, you will be able to fool your mind into thinking that the fear it's feeling is wholly rational. This should rid you of your dextrophobia right up to the point when the torrent of molten lava reaches you.

---

[1] The composition of the 'greats' varies from country to country. In a survey taken by the British magazine *Hide!* in May 2002, it was determined that the only reasons for hiding that could truly number themselves among the 'greats' were:
a) the discovery of a fresh-water fish nailed to your front door
b) the news that every male inhabitant of an obscure village in Serbia Montenegro has renamed himself after you
c) any trauma relating to the wearing of a yashmak.

[2] Cf. the complementary *levophobia*.

*The edge of the Universe. (Universe not shown actual size. Colours may vary.)*

**Chronophobia** *A fear of time*
As we have seen in **Starting Out** (p. 12),[3] only in very special circumstances will you be able to escape from time. Granted, it has been demonstrated that astronauts coming back from the Moon have spent fractionally less time away than clocks on Earth believe they have. However, although the Moon would make a fabulous hiding place (particularly the dark side), reaching it does again require space flight (see Dextrophobia, above), something that is tricky to arrange at the best of times. Also, the venture would leave the chronophobic hider only fractionally less fearful. In the end, it might be best to try some aversion therapy: consider hiding inside a clock tower.

---

[3] If you haven't seen, you've skipped a bit, which is typical of modern attitudes to great literature – it's all pick and mix and dipping in and out and never giving the work the room it needs to breathe. Go back and read the book properly – not because there will be questions later (which there will), but for the good of your soul.

# PSYCHOBABBLE

*The Chronophobia Clock – part aversion therapy tool, part Turner Prize entry.*

**Panophobia** *A fear of everything*
For the hider who doesn't like to do things by halves (motto: 'There is everything to fear, including fear.'). A bit difficult to know what to do about this one. If you're a true panophobe, you would presumably find a solution to your ailment as terrifying as the disorder itself. Try to get a good night's sleep and maybe things will seem all right in the morning.

*'Maybe things will seem all right in the morning.'*

# SCENES FROM THE WORLD OF SECLUSION

**nr 35. Pipe Ahoy**

*Renewable Energy Disasters No. 4: At the Blyth offshore wind farm, unevenly matched turbines cause the horizon to tilt.*

# 24. REVENGE OF THE FIFTY-FOOT HERRING

Herring Lane Car Park, Herring Lane, Spalding, Lincolnshire

**NEED to KNOW:** Spalding sits towards the edge of the Fens, at an equivalent point to which you could reasonably expect an unnecessary key change in a pop song that has run out of ideas after the third chorus. It is a town that welcomes motorised transport, catering for it with an endless series[1] of car parks. The least you can do is flock to one, though of course not in any sort of motorised transport since that would require you to leave a number-plated vehicle near your hiding place, which is a bit of a giveaway.

**ADVANTAGES:** It was a smart move of yours to take the bicycle instead, because there are no fewer than eight spaces reserved in which to leave it. Now, as unobtrusively as you can, saunter the 30 yards past the three mystical doorways and on to the Maidenhair Tree (which, if you're interested, was introduced from China and is a species of tree with no living relatives) and the sort of enchanted forest towards the back, and ease yourself in between the greenery and the satisfyingly ancient wall. Splendid.

**HAZARDS:** A stern warning sign declares that the car park is covered by CCTV. Don't panic yet. The chances are, no one's actually watching the neo-realistic film *Herring Lane – A Car Park* in real time and, if they are, all they have seen is a cyclist locking up a bicycle and disappearing into a plant. Cyclists are known to do this all the time, especially in French films, so no one will bat an eye. Furthermore, the CCTV business could work in your favour since it would be barmy to hide in full view of the cameras. Lets just let them think that.

[1] Not literally endless, that would be ridiculous.

**LOCAL KNOWLEDGE:** Sir Isaac Newton (gravity, differential calculus, apples) and Alfred, Lord Tennyson ('Break, break, break') were both members of The Gentleman's Society, which was founded in Spalding in 1710 so that local gentlemen could get together and talk about archaeology and read *The Tatler*. Understandably, it's not the thriving hub of the town it once was.

**FREE FOOD:** There's some white mustard growing here (yellow flowers, green leaves – the plant that's not the hawk's-beard next to it) which ought to be edible given its name, and is. Cook it if you must, but both leaves and flowers can be eaten raw, and very scrummy they are too.

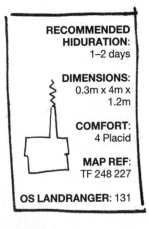

**RECOMMENDED HIDURATION:**
1–2 days

**DIMENSIONS:**
0.3m x 4m x 1.2m

**COMFORT:**
4 Placid

**MAP REF:**
TF 248 227

**OS LANDRANGER:** 131

**SUPPLIES:** The shopping streets of Spalding, though commendably close at hand, are not ones to send the heart skipping into the fields of Elysium. You might do best to visit Vine Street's 'Bookmark' (0.1 miles) which sells books (can't eat those), has a fountain (can't eat that), and offers a reading room (can't eat that) and a café (bingo).

**PUBLIC CONVENIENCES:** On Vine Street (0.1 miles), just opposite Abbey Passage. In common with the rest of Spalding, they don't open very late.

**COMPROMISED?** Try *23. The Quatrefoil Tower* (57 miles).

*The three mystical doorways that lead to ultimate self-knowing. Go through the incorrect one and you could get to know your wrong self. Best leave them bricked up.*

# 25. THE FAKENESS OF THINGS

Wigan Pier, Leeds and Liverpool Canal, Wigan, Lancashire

**NEED TO KNOW:** 'England is a family with the wrong members in control', sniped a pith-wielding George Orwell in his seething state-of-the-nation rantathon *The Road to Wigan Pier*. Wisely, by the time the first part of the book was published he'd taken himself off to Spain to fight in the Civil War (on the losing side, natch) and thereby avoided the furore it unleashed. Lying down in the prow of a fake barge just across the canal from the pier, you might well be able to put yourself in the shoes of one or two of those wrong family members – perhaps the uncle who ran a bingo scam that held the entire north-east in terror, or the grandmother who knitted the jumper that asphyxiated Leeds.

**ADVANTAGES:** You can be pretty certain that however bad a skipper you are, you have little chance of accidentally ramming this barge into a surfacing nuclear submarine and sparking a premature Armageddon.

**HAZARDS:** Coping with the disappointment of the whole fake barge business. Also, none of your friends think you capable of sparking a premature Armageddon, even if you had a proper barge at your disposal in which the heads of state of all the NATO-member nations were being held at gunpoint.

**ESSENTIALS:**

**LOCAL KNOWLEDGE:** It is a truth universally acknowledged (see also *8. Royal Crescent Garden*) that no southerner knows what Wigan Pier is. Indeed, since Orwell's title is the only thing the jesses know about Wigan (though it must be admitted that this is not altogether an undesirable state of consciousness), it comes as something of a surprise to discover that the town isn't on the coast. Furthermore, a little-known piece of legislation rushed through parliament during World War II makes it illegal for an explanation of what the pier actually is to be published in a book knowingly offered for sale south of Coventry.

**FREE FOOD:** Get in touch with 1930s Wigan and go hungry for a couple of decades.

**SUPPLIES:** The gift shop at the Wigan Pier Experience (yes, you heard right – come to terms with it now and the gag reflex will be under control by the time you visit) will supply you with fudge, Victory Vs and mint balls with a joy that might terrify at first glance.

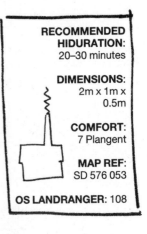

**RECOMMENDED HIDURATION:**
20–30 minutes

**DIMENSIONS:**
2m x 1m x 0.5m

**COMFORT:**
7 Plangent

**MAP REF:**
SD 576 053

**OS LANDRANGER:** 108

**PUBLIC CONVENIENCES:** The same Experience boasts some of the best examples of toiletry within sight of Wigan Pier and, for a down payment of £5.50 (£4.50 for locals, though I suppose they could just pop home and use their own), they are yours for the day. Excellent museum attached.

**READING MATTER:** Just don't get caught here reading *The Road to Wigan Pier* unless you want to find yourself transported into a parallel universe containing nothing but clichés.

COMPROMISED? Aim to be down and out in *62. Everyday is Like Sunday* (38 miles) by nightfall.

This Is The Site Of Wigan Pier

*Not at all a disappointment.*

King Street, Knutsford, Cheshire

**NEED to KNOW:** What will happen here on Earth when it's your turn to give up the ghost? Will a subscription be held among the grief-stricken populace of your home town so that a tower may be built on the High Street as a memorial to your greatness? Certainly your distribution of the Tower Memorial collecting boxes in readiness for your departure is a good first step, but I'd get something down in writing if I were you just to make absolutely sure. Of course, if you were Elizabeth Gaskell, you would be saved all this fretting since she has managed to get her own posthumous tower without even dropping any hints. Better still, right next door, across a narrow alleyway, there is a hole in a wall giving on to a gap. Gaps (or 'interstices' as hiders and Samuel Johnson prefer to call them) are the stuff of concealment and this is one of the best in the country. Settle yourself here and you're made for life. Which is why you really want to have your townsfolk sign on the dotted line now, so you can rest in peace until you rest in peace.

**ADVANTAGES:** The tower was once the power base of Knutsford Urban District Council. Thankfully, it's now an exclusive brasserie and hotel frequented by the sort of discreet clientele who would find the idea of searching for someone a touch indecorous. Furthermore, Knutsford is the model for Mrs Gaskell's *Cranford*, a deeply feminised town whose inhabitants, should your presence be detected, are likely to take pity on you and keep your sojourn 'neath the shadow of the tower the darkest of secrets (at least until chapter six).

**HAZARDS:** Narrow and very difficult to get into. Even harder to leave, especially after cramp has set in. Squishing a very real possibility. Also, pigeons perch above looking shifty and nervous, the least happy of combinations.

**LOCAL KNOWLEDGE:** Even for a 19th-century life, Elizabeth Gaskell was uncommonly surrounded by death. She was barely a year old when her mother died. Her brother disappeared either on the way to India or while there and was never heard of again. Then her father died. At 23, her first baby was still-born and a few years later her son died. For all that, she seemed to stay remarkably cheery. Also, she wrote a cracking biography of her friend, the acclaimed umlautist Charlotte Brontë. A good egg all round, really.

**FREE FOOD:** Anything the good people of Knutsford throw there. Likely to be high-class nosh but, at the end of the day, still leftovers. Let your stomach decide.

**RECOMMENDED HIDURATION:**
Indefinite

**DIMENSIONS:**
2m x 0.3m

**COMFORT:**
8 Plaguey

**MAP REF:**
SJ 752 786

**OS LANDRANGER:** 118

**SUPPLIES:** King Street is fit to burst with classy little shops eager to cater to your every squished whim.

**PUBLIC CONVENIENCES:** Just a hundred yards away in the car park at the end of Cotton Shop Yard.

**READING MATTER:** A life of St Godelina, or any other divine who found sainthood in immurement.

COMPROMISED? Try 25. *The Fakeness of Things* (20 miles).

*'You have not got that town in your map of Ireland; but Bonus Bernardus non videt omnia, as the Proverbia say.'*

# HOW NOT TO DIE

The last thing you want to do while hiding is take your eye off the ball and end up pushing up the daisies you were meant to be crouching behind. Although 'Cause of death: Hiding' is still a mercifully rare entry in the registers of county coroners, the possibility of a visit from the Grim Reaper while you're concentrating on other more pressing matters is one that must still be addressed.

Unless you have imprudently settled yourself down for the night under the shelter of a sleeping puma or on a rocky islet that disappears at high tide, the four most likely causes of your demise are the two hypothermias, along with dehydration and starvation. Against these, your weapons are warmth, water and food. However, the key is knowing how to use your weapons – after all, if you're in a cold breeze, you might not necessarily get much warmer throwing tins of artichoke hearts at the wind. In these circumstances, of course, it would be much more advisable to build a windbreak from the tins and wait for the gusts to abate.

**Exposure hypothermia**
*Solution*: This sort of hypothermia is caused by becoming too darn cold for your own good. The obvious solution is to select a nice snug hiding place out of the wind and rain (see **Building Your Own Hiding Place**, p. 18). If you have done this and you still feel the temperature of your body core plunging, don't just sit there shivering, put on some more dry clothes. No good? How about building a fire? Check first to see if there are any electrical sockets in the immediate vicinity before constructing one of the three-bar variety. If you're out of luck, and there are no gas bottles about either, you might want to hazard a wooden fire. There are many ways of building a successful fire from wood but you probably don't know any of them. Thankfully, full instructions are given in the Countryside Code. In no circumstances give in to the temptation to set yourself alight. Although this will keep you warm in the short term, it will have serious repercussions for your mid-to-long-term existence potential.

**Immersion hypothermia**
*Solution*: This sort of hypothermia is caused by becoming too darn cold for your own good while in some sort of liquid, typically water. This is a rather more serious proposition than exposure hypothermia since all the time you are immersed in, say, water, it's busily conducting heat away from your body at 25 times the rate that air would. The obvious solution, of course, is to get out of the water and wrap a nice warm towel around you. If this is not possible for some reason – you're floating hundreds of miles out to sea, for example – you should *not* start swimming about or treading water in a

frenzied manner since this will only leave you exhausted and thus prone to chill even faster. In the event that you also find yourself unable to light a fire, even with storm-proof matches and tinder that's been really really dried out first, an especially good weep will often help as you slide into unconsciousness.

*This fire was built in 30 minutes using the natural resources you might find in any typical wood.*

### Dehydration
*Solution*: Drink some water. If you have no water, do *not* drink your own urine. Not only is this a nasty habit, it also doesn't work for some reason. Nor should you drink someone else's urine for this also will not work.

### Starvation
*Solution*: Eat some food. Almost anything will do but you might want to stay off chillies for a bit if you can help it, unless you can find something to wash them down with (*not* your own urine – see above).

# 27. THE CAVE IN THE HILL

**Wettonmill, Manifold Valley, Staffordshire**

**NEED to KNOW:** A teasingly tricky cave to locate – invisible from below, in the same way that a ha-ha is indiscernible from the drawing room of a country house, and barely perceptible from above. It features a partially sheltered porch section, two trees, and an inner quarters large enough for one prone (or supine) adult and a basic set of surgical instruments. Your predecessors here include Iron Age hermits and, for one night only, fleeing Jacobites.

**ADVANTAGES:** Almost the perfect hiding place since there is nothing to indicate to unwelcome pursuers that it, and therefore you, are here at all.

**HAZARDS:** The psychological effects of spending any length of time in a place which appears not to exist in any meaningful sense have, as yet, not been fully researched (though residents of Telford may beg to differ). If, by the fourth day, you begin to undergo out-of-body experiences in which you look down at yourself only to discover you are not there, it may be time to move on.

## ESSENTIALS:

**LOCAL KNOWLEDGE:** Going by the tracks in the mud in the porch section, it would appear that sheep occasionally frequent the cave. However, there is no evidence to suggest that they do anything more than spend a few minutes mildly surprised by an out-of-mutton experience before leaving to carry on with their sheepy lives, their world view changed forever.

**FREE FOOD:** Herb robert, not a nourishing meal in and of itself but very effective in the treatment of ulcers and wounds. This may be of some consolation when you find you cannot eat because of the raging pain of a ruptured duodenal ulcer.

**SUPPLIES:** The National Trust tea rooms just below at Wettonmill are perfect if you can attune your body to a diet entirely composed of scones, ice cream and Earl Grey tea.

**PUBLIC CONVENIENCES:** The toilets situated in the Wetton car park (1 mile) are open 24 hours a day but are not the ideal place for self-surgery on, say, a ruptured duodenal ulcer. Wetton is the setting for the annual international toe-wrestling championships, so expect bother.

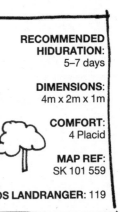

**RECOMMENDED HIDURATION:**
5–7 days

**DIMENSIONS:**
4m x 2m x 1m

**COMFORT:**
4 Placid

**MAP REF:**
SK 101 559

**OS LANDRANGER:** 119

## MAKING A QUICK GETAWAY:

**BUS:** A hike north to the village of Warslow (2 miles) is a natural precursor to bus trips to Buxton, Ashbourne, Sheffield, Leek, Bakewell and, twice a week, Hanley, the one town of the five in Stoke that anyone can name with any certainty.

**OTHER:** A mobility scooter is now available, though only for use on the Tissington Trail.

**COMPROMISED?** Try *28. Not Errwood Hall* (13 miles).

*Hills – lovely in the wild, but far too cumbersome for the average lounge.*

# 28. NOT ERRWOOD HALL

nr Errwood Reservoir, Goyt Valley, Buxton, Derbyshire

**NEED to KNOW:** This ancient dry-stone wall is now shrouded by a huge rhododendron planted by the world-travelling Grimshawe family of Errwood Hall. Of course, it's possible that it self-seeded and they didn't plant it there at all, but one imagines that that would only delight the long-departed Grimshawes all the more. The steps up and over the wall bear witness, if witness were required, to the ghost of an ancient thoroughfare that passed from east(ish) to west(ish). The trail has now moved south, thus making the steps redundant for all purposes but your own.

**ADVANTAGES:** By simply rolling underneath the rhododendron and lying quite still, there's no reason why anyone should ever disturb you at all until your peaceful cadaver is reported on the regional news as having been discovered by a man walking his dog. This should come as no surprise really, since men walking their dogs are forever finding dead bodies under bushes – indeed it's a wonder they dare leave the house with their beloved mutts in tow. If they do so in the hope of someday coming across the FA Cup under a hedge, they would do well to remember that such an event occurs just once a century on average. Indeed, they have far more chance of *playing* in the FA Cup, an event that occurs annually and involves hundreds of teams from all parts of the country.

**HAZARDS :** There's a fair-to-even chance that, should it ever rain in Britain again, some of it will cascade down the hill onto your prone (or possibly supine) self. You should not take this personally – it is simply nature's way of making sure we all bathe at least once a year (like Elizabeth I, whether we need to or not).

**LOCAL KNOWLEDGE:** Do not give in to the temptation to hide in the Victoriana ruinara of nearby Errwood Hall. Derbyshire's answer to Machu Picchu it may be, but good hiding territory it is not. So ruined is it that you are very likely to be unearthed by the first sightseer with any sight to see.

**FREE FOOD:** As far as has been established, no part of the rhododendron is edible. However, science is forever pressing forwards, so there's no knowing whether parts of the rhododendron, as yet unknown, might be discovered by future biologists and that one or more of these might be edible. In the meantime, bring sandwiches.

**RECOMMENDED HIDURATION:**
2–4 days

**DIMENSIONS:**
3m x 3m

**COMFORT:**
5 Plain

**MAP REF:**
SK 006 748

**OS LANDRANGER:** 119

**SUPPLIES:** In summer, a pricey ice-cream van in the car park by Errwood Reservoir (0.25 miles) will sell you pricey ice creams. Try to ignore the circling packs of dog-walkers eyeing you like vultures.

**PUBLIC CONVENIENCES:** It's 3 miles to Buxton and uphill for most of it.

COMPROMISED? Try *26. The Mrs Gaskell Memorial Tower was my Neighbour* (19 miles).

*A balloonist (not pictured) spies your hiding place (centre). He suspects nothing. He lands in a field in Cheshire. He returns home as if nothing had happened.*

# ROBERT THE BRUCE
## (1274–1329)

> **Hiduration**: 9 months
> **Value as role model**: 7/10

On 5 June 1306, Robert the Bruce was excommunicated by Pope Clement V. This was no bad thing, really, since in medieval times you couldn't really go about calling yourself a proper renegade if you hadn't been excommunicated at least once. Furthermore, rather than being cast out from the Mother Church on a namby-pamby technicality such as a dalliance with some unorthodox view of the Atonement, Robert the Bruce had just gone right ahead and killed someone. In a church. Bit of a no-no, that, in the Middle Ages. The someone in question – fellow Scot, John 'Red' Comyn – also happened to be a chum of King Edward (the First, though for obvious reasons no one bothered calling him that at the time). Pope Clement V, meanwhile, just happened to be from Bordeaux, a city that just happened to be subject to the English Crown, which just happened at the time to be on the head of King Edward.

Edward himself had just held a very jolly feast in London at which his son (Edward II, though not for another 21 months so hold your horses) was invested as Duke of Aquitaine. After all the back-slapping and sword-waggling, Edward (the First, etc. etc.) produced some live swans sporting a plethora of gold chains. He then swore 'before God and the Swans to avenge the death of Comyn'. No one had thought to swear before swans before, and certainly not ones sporting bling, and it rather set a trend for the remainder of the Middle Ages.

Anyway, we digress. The upshot of all this murdering and excommunicating and swan-swearing – and a bruising defeat just outside Perth when the perfidious English refused to obey the chivalric codes of war – was that Robert found it opportune to make himself scarce for a bit.

He took to the mountains with about 500 men, that being the pitiful remnant of his army. While Edward was busy declaring them outlaws – a sort of sentence of death *in absentia* – they lived for weeks on nothing but meat and water. As they moved west, the killing continued: salmon, trout and eels, none of whom were English, were all slaughtered, which seems a bit unfair.

However, aside from one awkward moment when they were ambushed by a much larger force led by the understandably peeved John MacDougall (aka Red Comyn's son-in-law), the outlaws managed to stay out of harm's way. Eventually they found themselves rowing a little armada of galleys over to the Mull of Kintyre, where they unhappily discovered they were being pursued by an English fleet. They thus set off for Ireland but got swept onto the island of Rathlin, just off Antrim. Here the trail goes cold – appropriately enough, since it was winter by then – and little is known of Robert until spring, which finds him attempting to hide in the lands of Carrick in south-west Scotland. Here, according to a number of probably apocryphal accounts, he kept getting attacked by groups of three men whom he was forced to kill with mighty blows of his sword. This must have been irksome, but no worse than knowing that his rather over-faithful bloodhound, captured by the MacDougalls, was being used by the English to track him down. This compelled him to keep crossing rivers and streams in order to avoid the beast, and just goes to prove once more the superiority of cats as pets.

To cut a long and arduous story short, Robert eventually enlarged his band of warriors to such an extent that he was able to come out of hiding and start killing people again. He was so good at this that he managed to remain King of Scotland the rest of his days. Amen.

> **Lesson**: Learn from the spider – if at first you don't succeed: hide, bide your time, then come back and kill lots of English people.

## 29. THE M1

**Misk Hill, Hucknall, Nottinghamshire**

**NEED to KNOW:** A footbridge carries a remote and ill-frequented footpath across Britain's first motorway. By the simple expedient of lying flat on the bridge, the hider is out of sight of all those scurrying by below.

**ADVANTAGES:** Even drivers high up in the cabs of those uncompromisingly vast articulated lorries that make the country such a joy to live in will be no more aware of your presence than they are of the sands that trickle remorselessly down through the hour-glass of their restless existence.

**HAZARDS:** There is always the risk of being spied upon from above by balloonists. In the event of irksome balloonular activity, drape yourself in yellow. It is very difficult to judge scale from above, and any latter-day Montgolfierians will probably take you for a poorly placed banana.

**ESSENTIALS:**

**LOCAL KNOWLEDGE:** This section of the M1 was opened in May 1967, thus enabling Londoners to reach Pinxton without let, hindrance or concern as to whether Pinxton itself was merely an invention of some town planner's post-World Cup fevered mind.

**FREE FOOD:** Don't attempt to reach the hawthorn berries between the footbridge and the motorway unless you intend to become a minor item on a regional news broadcast preceded by the words: 'Some viewers may find the following images distressing.' (See also 'body found under bushes by man walking dog': *28. Not Errwood Hall*.)

**SUPPLIES**: Jayne's General Store, Nabb's Lane (1 mile). Don't let the fact that the shop is in Hucknall tempt you into asking if they sell simply bread.

**PUBLIC CONVENIENCES**: The occasional Portaloo might well pass below but will, in all but the most exceptional circumstances, be moving too fast to be of any practical use.

## MAKING A QUICK GETAWAY:

**TRAIN**: Those choosing to flee to Nottingham or Worksop can do so from Hucknall station, several times a day if needs be.

**RECOMMENDED HIDURATION:**
4–6 hours

**DIMENSIONS:**
50m x 2m x 18cm

**COMFORT:**
9 Playful

**MAP REF:**
SK 502 492

**OS LANDRANGER** 129

**OTHER**: A frequent tram service on the Nottingham Express Transit from Station Road, Hucknall (2.5 miles) transits all and sundry in an expressive fashion 10 miles south to Nottingham like something emerging from a time warp not entirely of its own making.

## COMPROMISED? Try *23. The Quatrefoil Tower* (22 miles).

*Four chimneys, four Horsemen of the Apocalypse – the maths is simple.*

# 30. SOME SORT OF BUILDING

Spurn Point, at the end of Spurn Head, nr Kilnsea, Humberside

**NEED to KNOW:** Imagine dreaming that Humberside had a crooked finger that it extended into the North Sea as if about to launch into an Alvin Stardust hit while upside down. Spurn Point would then be very much the fingernail of your (more or less harmless but don't go there too often) reverie. *Some Sort of Building* is just at the bottom of the white bit of the fingernail but only if the nail itself is on the other side to that traditionally favoured by the cuticle portion of the finger. In less digital terms, go to (nearly) the end of Spurn Point and it's on your left. As its name suggests, *Some Sort of Building* was once just that (probably *Some Sort of Military Building*). Its very lack of fixed purpose nowadays is the essence of its brilliance as a place of seclusion since no one is really likely to bother with it unless they are hiding themselves, and the chances of you wishing to hide there at the same time as someone else are scanty. Good news for you: bad news for lovers of architectural purpose.

**ADVANTAGES:** It's a sort of building so, assuming you habitually inhabit a building yourself (any sort will do), you should feel quite at home here.

**HAZARDS:** Spurn Head is not what you might call a fixed point, and has been heading west of late. Half a mile or so to the east – where today there is just sea – there was once a village called Ravenser Odd. The tiny sandy island on which Odd stood sort of rose up out of the sea around 1234, became a thriving port with its own MP and everything, and then vanished again around 1366. Fourteen other villages the length of the Head have come and gone as the ground beneath them has pushed west, so do check with local people first if you intend to hide here for more than a few centuries.

## ESSENTIALS:

**LOCAL KNOWLEDGE:** A 7th-century hermit called St Wilgils (feast day: 31 January) is the first known occupant of Spurn Head. He had a son, St Willibrord (the apostle to the Fresians, but I expect you knew that), so presumably he wasn't a hermit all the time.

**SUPPLIES:** There is Some Sort of Café in a Portakabin just a halloo away but it's a tad fair-weathery.

**PUBLIC CONVENIENCES:** A long lonely trudge back to the Blue Bell car park (6 miles).

COMPROMISED? Try *31. Bile Bean Hole* (56 miles).

**RECOMMENDED HIDURATION:**
1–2 days

**DIMENSIONS:**
3m x 5m x 3m

**COMFORT:**
3 Pleasant

**MAP REF:**
TA 402 111

**OS LANDRANGER:** 113

*Spurn Lighthouse: 128 feet high, 145 steps, 300,000 bricks. Decommissioned in 1985 just two years after top Sheffield beat combo Pulp released 'My Lighthouse'. Pathos is everywhere.*

# HOW TO HIDE IN A TREE (I)

Taxonomists – on the whole a fussy pedantic lot for whom a split hair is a thing of beauty – may manhandle you into a corner of a room and tell you otherwise, but deep down even they know that Nature can roughly be divided into three categories: tree, shrub and flower. As anyone who has ever been to school, even once, knows, these three can be defined as follows.

**A Tree is a leg with a Shrub on top.**

**A Shrub is a Tree without a leg.**

**A Flower is a bit of loose Shrub.**

An imperfect but otherwise helpful rule of thumb with regard to the Three Types of Nature is as follows.

**A Flower is of little use to the hider; a Shrub may be of some use, if it is a big Shrub; but a Tree is nearly always handy.**

It behoves every would-be hider to commit this to memory before they commit themselves to a forget-me-not (however large).

In order not to encourage the sort of half-hearted hiding that the scanty cover afforded by flowers and the great majority of shrubs provokes, we shall pass them by without comment and head for the trees. Here we find ourselves faced with a conundrum: what class of tree is best for hiding?

## Deciduous vs evergreen vs invertebrate

### Deciduous
As their Latin root – *deciduus* ('fall') – suggests, these trees are apt to fall over (see *5. Eeyore's Gloomy Place*), so be very careful. Furthermore, even when they remain upright, their leaves tend to drop off around autumn time, a course of action that invariably results in a sort of skeletal version of a proper tree that is of no use to man or beast. Such trees should therefore be selected for concealment purposes only from late spring to early autumn. Outside of these times, you will have to come disguised as a branch and lie very still.

### Evergreen
The clue is in the word: *ever* ('for some considerable time') *green* ('a green thing'; 'the colour of a greenfinch'; 'a person with little experience'). These trees very rarely fall over or ever lose their leaves, both of which facets make for first-rate camouflage for green things such as greenfinches or people with little experience. A greenfinch new to hiding could probably conceal itself in an evergreen almost indefinitely. Even if you are not a greenfinch – and in today's globally warmed Britain fewer and fewer of us are – an evergreen is still your best friend when you need to disappear for a while. If it is said that a man 'cannot see the wood for the trees' you can be pretty sure it is because those trees are evergreens.

### Invertebrate
Be suspicious of any tree claiming to be invertebrate: it is almost certainly attempting to pull the wool over your eyes.

**NB** As discussed elsewhere in books, the best place to hide a leaf is a tree, so if you have any leaves that need hiding, do bring them along with you and so experience the satisfaction of killing two birds with one stone.

# 31. BILE BEAN HOLE

Lord Mayor's Walk, York, Yorkshire

**NEED to KNOW:** Pick up almost any British magazine from the mid 1960s and in the small ads section towards the back you'll find the middle-aged Mrs P.F. of Hants beaming out at you with what appears to be some ill-fitting false teeth and a ring doughnut haircut. 'I feel fit and well … look younger …', she glows. How so? Well, she's just taken some Bile Beans and is now, as the advert's (groovy all-lower-case headline) assures us, 'freed from constipation'. Good news all round. In fact, so relieved is Mrs P.F. that the folk at Bile Beans would have us believe that she took the trouble to write in to them to let them know of her successful bowel movement. The only cautionary note is sounded at the end: 'Take Bile Beans and correct constipation overnight'. I don't know about you, but 'overnight' is not really the time I want to discover that my constipation has suddenly been corrected. Perhaps this explains their disappearance from the British market.

**ADVANTAGES:** As you nestle down in the verdant undergrowth, musing on the '11 active ingredients carefully formulated to give *thorough* relief', you might just glimpse the top of York Minster and have your thoughts redirected to higher things.

**HAZARDS:** In fact you'd be well advised to have your mind elsewhere because, frankly, it's a nasty place to be. Just what drives the people of York to take rubbish from their homes and hide it among shrubbery? And who left the pair of Sean the Sheep slippers here?

102

**LOCAL KNOWLEDGE:** York is reputed to be the most haunted city in Britain per capita (of live inhabitants, presumably). The pick of the phantoms are the Roman centurions who, with an eye to detail that does them much credit, are only ever seen from the knee up because the level of Roman York was a calf-and-ankle lower than today's city. If you are hiding here at night and find yourself indisposed by the apparition of a phalanx of three-quarter-length Roman soldiery, you can at least take comfort in the fact that thousands of Bile Beans customers have been there before you.

**SUPPLIES:** Mary Shortle's doll-heavy toy shop just across the road might well be able to supply you with food but it's likely to be very tiny and made of wood, so you might do better to try one of York's many shops that specialise in full-size non-wooden food.

**IF IT ALL GETS TOO MUCH:** The Micklegate Run consists of downing a drink in every inn on Micklegate, reputedly the most pub-laden street in England. This constitutes the *other* sure-fire way of voiding your bowel in the least time possible.

**RECOMMENDED HIDURATION:**
2–4 hours

**DIMENSIONS:**
3m x 3m x 2m

**COMFORT:**
8 Plaguey

**MAP REF:**
SE 606 524

**OS LANDRANGER:** 105

## MAKING A QUICK GETAWAY :

**TRAIN:** The nearby railway station (0.75 miles) was once the biggest in Europe. Huzzah.

**COMPROMISED?** Try *32. Behind the Gentlemen* (28 miles).

*Fly tipping – in my day we contented ourselves with getting a fly, putting a heavy weight on one of its wings and watching it fall over.*

# 32. BEHIND THE GENTLEMEN

Gentlemen, Rosedale Abbey, North Yorkshire Moors, Yorkshire

**NEED TO KNOW:** Good hidingness is an art *and* a science, a lesson the hider neglects to learn at his or her peril. Sometimes mere art alone will just not do, and this is where such venues as the public conveniences in the village of Rosedale Abbey come in. Banal, yes, but remember that banality may sometimes prove your best friend, even if not one with whom you would want to spend an entire weekend at a lakeside retreat. The twist in this case is that you hide not *in* the toilets, a strategy fraught with danger, but just *behind* them. Simple yet brilliant.

**ADVANTAGES:** In tests, not a single member of the public, when asked where they would search for someone, declared that they would look behind the entrance to the gentlemen's convenience in Rosedale Abbey.

**HAZARDS:** The North Yorkshire Moors may include the largest continuous area of heather moorland in England but they are also famous for the intermittent fits of blusteriness and intemperance to which they are heir, and there are times when weather will come down off the hills and attack you with what will seem like wooden kitchen implements. Although you are entirely sheltered from the road by a good stout stone wall, your back is protected only by a few twiggy-like things and a sort of gap that presumably used to be a fence. Arm yourself with a stout stone umbrella or some very strong mints.

## ESSENTIALS:

**LOCAL KNOWLEDGE:** Apart from a few bits and pieces, the abbey after which the village is named no longer exists, so there's no chance of covering your trail even further by becoming a nun, however much you've flirted with the idea in the past.

104

**SUPPLIES:** Mints of all sorts can be purchased at the Abbey Stores or the Rosedale Bakery and General Stores (both a hop and a skip away). A chess game packed in a tin is also available at the Abbey Stores and no doubt it would cheer them up quite considerably if you took it off their hands.

**PUBLIC CONVENIENCES:** Well, you're there, really.

**IF IT ALL GETS TOO MUCH:** The village flaunts a brace of tea rooms not a hundred yards from where you are being attacked by wooden kitchen implements. Clean off the blood and order a nice pot of lapsang souchong.

**RECOMMENDED HIDURATION:**
2–4 hours

**DIMENSIONS:**
2m x 3m

**COMFORT:**
5 Plain

**MAP REF:**
SE 724 960

**OS LANDRANGER:** 100

**MAKING A QUICK GETAWAY:**

**TRAIN:** The North Yorkshire Moors Railway runs a good part of the year and links with so-called proper rail services at Grosmont. All *you* need to do is hike the 8 miles or so across the moors to either Newton Dale or Goathland. The latter stood in as Hogsmeade station for some film or other, so you may favour Newton Dale in order to avoid the location anoraks.

**COMPROMISED?** Try *34. Your Office in the Woods* (43 miles).

*Two walls and some grass – Shakespeare would have made an entire tragedy out of it. What will you do?*

# PLANT LIFE AND HOW TO EAT IT

There comes a time in every hider's life when the thought of a dinner consisting entirely of blackberries and rainwater no longer raises the pulse to the ecstatic cadences of old. If this time should coincide with the knocking up of a tasty smackerel courtesy of a serendipitously beached crate of Fortnum and Mason's provisions, all well and good. However, if the crisis comes when the hider has only a handful of blackberries and a puddle between her and starvation as night draws on, something will inevitably give.

Giving is obviously a good thing and – in the form in which nothing is expected in return – is the last truly counter-cultural activity in which one can engage in a society that has come to value possessions over all else. However, the something that inevitably gives is a different kettle of fish altogether, and one that can be tackled only by the application of culinary guile.

Thankfully, guile is not what it used to be. Whereas once it could be acquired only through years of practice at stealth and cunning, today it can be the prized possession of the most innocent of ingénues simply by applying these easy-to-grasp recipes to ingredients obtainable from any half-decent acre of British soil. As our continental cousins have it: 'May the *cordon bleu*[1] be with in which and something something.'

**Nettle soup**
Nettles, aside from providing a habitat for careful butterflies, are your friends. Making sure to employ some sort of sting-proof barrier (crêpe paper, for instance, is both effective and pretty), pluck some choice tender sprigs, and hold them out in the rain for a bit to cleanse them before tossing them light-heartedly into your pot. Boil them for a while, have a go at liquidising them, and eat piping hot. For an even scrummier soup, add wild onions, hedge garlic, a dab of cornflour, a smidge of milk and a flick of seasoning. Where nettles are scarce, substitute with mallow leaves or a can of soup.

**Laver bread**
Harvested by going to where it's growing and just picking it up and putting it into your pockets, laver (or *lawr* if picked up and put in pockets in Wales) is a sort of shiny black seaweed. Unlike other thick seaweeds such as bladder-wrack, laver is easily identified since it is just one cell in breadth.

[1] Lit. 'blue rope' (after the bluey-coloured rope that is considered a delicacy in northern France).

*In the reality-television series* What's Wrong With The Hargreaves?, *this patch of nettles fed and clothed the plucky east London family for over a year.*

Take all that bladderwrack out of your pockets and start again. Be sure to leave the fronds in place on the rocks so that the laver keeps growing long after you have succumbed to bladderwrack poisoning, and take the glossy leaves back to your seaside lair. Here you may dry the laver before eating it, as a Japanese person might do, or dice it and add it to your nettle soup, as most non-Japanese races of the world prefer. If you are Welsh you may make it into *bara lawr* or laver bread by bottling it and selling it to tourists.

Not to be confused with real bread or lava.

### Chestnut stew
A versatile meal that can be enjoyed at all times of year but is best prepared around October when chestnuts can be added for that extra chestnutty flavour. Of which, horse chestnuts can be eaten at a pinch but only after a lot of faffing around and boiling and drying and grating and whatnot and even then they taste ghastly so they're best left to small rodents who have all winter to cook and prepare them.

Scour the ground for the sweet chestnuts (those still on the tree will not be ripe so you can put that stick down) and, once located, prize them from their prickly shells. The crêpe paper that served you so well with the nettles is of dubious value for this procedure. Indeed, the only sure-fire method of not having your fingers perforated by nature's little acupuncturists is to have someone else do the prizing.

*Rudimentary pot made from two tin cans. Note fine beading work and designer handle (optional).*

Once you, or an accommodating other, have accumulated sufficient mounds of the burnished little chaps, fashion a rudimentary pot out of empty tin cans or similar, build a fire and boil the chestnuts for twenty minutes.

While you're waiting, find a pint of good vegetable stock and add to it some potatoes, carrots, tomatoes, cauliflower, broccoli, onions, courgettes, yellow and red peppers, fresh (not tinned) artichoke hearts, yams, half a level teaspoon of black molasses (Cuban if you can get it), tomato purée, chopped dates, a pinch each of nutmeg and paprika, a splash of mango juice (fairly traded where possible), two pinches of turmeric, a teaspoon of Dijon mustard (though any sufficiently peppery mustard will do), three sprigs of rosemary, a good shake of lime juice, a teaspoon of dessert wine (not German) and a swirl of single cream. Decorate with a floret of parsley and serve immediately.

The unpleasant acrid smell you will detect after your meal comes from the chestnuts that have now boiled dry.

## Dandelion wine
There's nothing so refreshing after a hot day's hiding than downing a quart or two of dandelion wine and sleeping the rest of the month off. All you need to do is choose a date seven weeks before a hot day's hiding, then go out and gather a host of golden dandelion blossoms, some hot water, a heap of sugar, a puff of wine yeast, a shilling's worth of nutrient, and sundry oranges and lemons chopped the size of the fragments typically left after a standard-issue hand grenade has been tossed into the tomb of King Xerxes by a nervous young lieutenant. Immerse the blossoms in the water, leave for 24 hours (book yourself into a hotel or something), strain through muslin, reheat, add the fruit, reheat again, transfer to a stone jar and allow to ferment for seven weeks, skimming daily. The resultant white wine is not only light and tangy with cheeky undertones of burdock and resin that bear comparison with the best thistle wines, it is also low in tannins, so in the event that you emerge from your coma you shouldn't have too much of a headache.

# 33. CAVERN OF THE WHALE

nr Rydal, Cumbria

**NEED to KNOW:** Many people think of caves as a relatively recent phenomenon, but this is in fact far from the truth. Caves have been known to exist in the Lake District for hundreds of years and this one is no exception. It has a wet floor, like a proper cave, and hundreds of years of history, though sadly it lacks the cave paintings one might expect in a cave, particularly one with sides like this one. The naturally forming stepping stones in the floor are a bit like art, I suppose, if only in a Tate Moderny sort of way. Drips can be experienced from nearly all parts of the ceiling, leaving just a few sparse dry patches to store your acrylics and brushes.

**ADVANTAGES:** There's a sort of inner bit inside the cave, like an enormous stony flap, which aids hiddenness to no small degree. Furthermore, the beginners-to-intermediate level of climbing ability required to shin up the rocks to the entrance will deter the vast majority of over-curious trippers. The acoustics of the cave are such that a mere sneeze inside sounds like the barking of a trapped whale calf from the outside. A few well-timed sneezes should deter the remainder of the over-curious.

**HAZARDS:** Under no circumstances should you attempt to hide in the Lake District. Even in the most remote parts, on the foulest winter day, you will be badgered by Keith and Candice-Marie types. Also, the mothers of whales will inevitably become attracted by your incessant sneezing and amble along to see what's what.

**LOCAL KNOWLEDGE:** It is inconceivable that Grasmere (1.2 miles) boy William Wordsworth (1770–1850 inclusive) would not have known this cave well, and anyone who says otherwise is clearly an unhinged e'er-do-ill. Nor can it be questioned that the final lines of his poem 'To Winter' were inspired by this particular cave: '... till heaven smiles, and the monster / Is driv'n yelling to his caves beneath mount Hecla.' The 'Hecla' here is evidently a reference to nearby Helvellyn (6 miles), a mount that manifestly starts with the same two letters, a common standard of 'that's about enough of a clue' in the poetic world.

**FREE FOOD:** Whale meat.

**RECOMMENDED HIDURATION:**
2–4 hours

**DIMENSIONS:**
30m x 10m x 20m

**COMFORT:**
6 Plebeian

**MAP REF:**
NY 355 058

**OS LANDRANGER:** 90

**SUPPLIES:** Shops at Grasmere will supply you amply with that which is not entirely necessitous but which glittereth much.

**PUBLIC CONVENIENCES:** At the car park on the Grasmere road (0.6 miles). No mirrors.

**COMPROMISED?** Try 38. *The Shelter of Cold Feet* (37 miles).

'I wander'd lonely as a clump. *No, that won't do. Wish I were back on Westminster Bridge – filthy as Hecla but at least you get a decent view. Now, let's see –* I wander'd lonely as a clod. *Yes! Like it.'*

# 34. YOUR OFFICE IN THE WOODS

The west bank of the River Wear, Durham, Co. Durham

**NEED to KNOW:** High up above the Wear, just along from the water mill, opposite the cathedral, off a path that leads nowhere, buried deep among the laurel trees is your office in the woods. A desk. A chair. A length of blue piping. What more could the aspiring businessperson possibly need to get a foothold on the vertical cliff face of Capitalism? Contrary to popular belief, office equipment such as telephones, computers and an internet connection are now considered outré by the gurus who sit at the cutting edge of the relentless Circular Saw of Destruction that is free enterprise. More important by far is a hacking away at costs, a slashing of liabilities, and the leaving of the shortest possible trail of breadcrumbs between you and the holy grail of commerce – zero start-up capital. In this office you will have no bills for anything. Your only outgoings are whatever you decide to pay yourself. It's the perfect business model. There is also some holly, which is jolly, and which saves expenditure when decorating the office for the Christmas party.

**ADVANTAGES:** The view of the cathedral is certain to inspire you and your employees as you reflect upon the Normans who built this massive edifice to strike fear and trembling into the untamed peoples of the north country. To think Norman is to think Success.

**HAZARDS:** The endless doleful two-note chimes of the cathedral bells are wont to keep one up at night. Also, it's possible that the office environment may fool you into getting too involved in the whole business thing, whereby you find yourself doing some paperwork by mistake. Remember, you are here to hide, not to feel guilty about that report for Mr Sheldon that should have been in last Friday and was the reason for you making yourself scarce in the first place.

**LOCAL KNOWLEDGE:** Durham is very old. Anyone you meet in the street who claims to be a founding father is almost certainly lying. The city made its fortune from Durham wheat, the single ingredient of such popular pastas as spaghetti, lasagne, macaroni and broccoli.

**FREE FOOD:** The delicate white flowers of the cherry laurel give forth the shiny purply oblong cherries that give the trees their name. Cherries also lend their name to cherry trees. The fruit of the latter is yummy, except when glacéed. The fruit of the former is yucky. Best to bring a baguette with you or pick up something at the office canteen.

**SUPPLIES:** Most of the shops in Durham are, of course, devoted to the sale of Durham wheat.
However, persevere and you will find other produce there such as oats, corn and, in season, laurel cherries.

**IF IT ALL GETS TOO MUCH:** During university holidays (i.e. all but a few weeks every year), you can stay more or less incognito in Durham Castle where they do a very reasonable B&B.

**RECOMMENDED HIDURATION:**
6–8 hours

**DIMENSIONS:**
2m x 4m x 3m

**COMFORT:**
2 Plummy

**MAP REF:**
NZ 272 422

**OS LANDRANGER:** 88

COMPROMISED? Try 35. *Pipe Ahoy* (24 miles).

*The one cathedral in England that can still be found growing out of a holly tree.*

# ROGUE MALE – GEOFFREY HOUSEHOLD
## (1900–88)

**Hiduration:** 3 weeks
**Value as role model:** 8/10

In the England of the 1920s–30s, there was only one literary genre: the adventure yarn. These habitually featured a high-born rugged individualist of unimpeachable ethical standards who thought nothing of squeezing a bullet out of his own shoulder and using it as a teat to wean an orphaned muntjac deer. John Buchan took it upon himself to write most of these books, but of course he couldn't be everywhere all the time so other lesser lights chipped in on occasion. One such was the improbably monikered Geoffrey Household –
one of the few authors to have a household name before he became one. Household's canny twist in *Rogue Male* was that his hero didn't actually have a name … then in the last few pages, after the story itself has finished, readers are led to believe that the account is autobiographical.

If this is so, we can deduce that Household was a member of the upper classes who, in 1939, travelled alone to Poland and came within a hair's breadth of assassinating an unnamed tyrant (but, since Polish president Ignacy Mościcki wasn't really in the tyrant class, you can take it as read that the target was one Adolf Hitler, presumably indulging in a bit of pre-invasion tourism). He was captured by secret service agents, tortured and left for dead. Naturally, he didn't die, but dragged himself away and escaped back to Britain posing as a recuperating schoolmaster on a sailing holiday. We've all done it, I suppose.

Sadly, his problems weren't to end there, and he soon found himself being pursued by any number of foreign agents, one of whom he was compelled to frazzle on the live rail at Aldwych underground station.[1] Eventually, after much harem-scarem and some upsetting scenes with a tandem and side-car, he went to ground in Dorset (see *3. Household in the Hills*). Quite literally as it happens, and this is where the novel serves as a useful primer for the budding hider. From it, we learn:

i. A burrow hewn from sandstone should have a door (preferably made to measure in nearby Beaminster) and a sort of ventilation shaft (which will also come into its own as a handy plot device later on).

ii. A stout barrier of thorns and nettles tends to dissuade folk from taking too keen an interest in your lair.

iii. Cob nuts, sloes and blackberries make a meal fit for a man.

iv. A cow will allow you to milk it by hand if you feed it enough salt.

v. A foreign agent lurking outside your burrow can be killed by building a ballista (a Roman artillery piece) out of bricks, bits of wood and the guts of a feral cat called Asmodeus that said agent has just shot and stuffed down the ventilation shaft into your burrow (which action has, coincidentally, made you a bit angry because the cat was your friend and you'd given him a pretentious Ancient Canaanite name and everything, and this has driven you to ditch your scruples and wreak bloody vengeance on the foreign swine), and using it to drive an iron spit through his stupid foreign forehead.

As it turns out, the story is not true. Geoffrey Household, when not writing his 37 novels, was actually a printers' ink salesman called Edward West. Even when he served in the Intelligence Corps in WWII he failed to carry out a single assassination attempt on Hitler. Fiction, huh? It's all made up, you know.

> **Lesson:** Foreigners are bad and you'll only ever feel really safe from them when your best friend is a ballista made out of the entrails of a dead cat.

[1] Note that Aldwych station is now closed, so you'll have to find some other way of dispatching shady foreign types.

# 35. PIPE AHOY

Cambois, nr Blyth, Northumberland

**NEED to KNOW:** The dunes at Cambois were used in a scene in the 1971 film *Get Carter*, the über-gritty gangland you-killed-my-brother revenge-fest in which the loveable north-east entirely comprises empty multi-storey car parks, disused warehouses, gloomy cafés, crumbling terraced houses, grime, shotguns and (briefly, for a bit of contrast) a minor stately home. If you want to do some research before arriving, it's the few seconds when Ian Hendry (Eric) is seen running away from Michael Caine (Jack). The dunes are still there but would do today's hider as much good as they did poor Eric, since none of the grass is above a foot high. Anyone loftier than that should make their way down to the beach and nestle under the ample sewage pipery.

**ADVANTAGES:** The view is just splendid. Then there's that whole juxtaposition of the pipe and the sea: the ugliness and the beauty; the created and the creation; the motionless and the restless; and the sewage-filled and the sewage-filled. Furthermore, you're out of the wind, and much wind there is, as evidenced by the two wind turbines half a mile out to sea. They were once the biggest in the world, you know, but no one can explain how they came to shrink.

**HAZARDS:** Dog walkers. Why do they do it?

**ESSENTIALS:**

LOCAL KNOWLEDGE: This used to be a nudist beach, apparently. Now it is not.

**FREE FOOD:** Since you are on such intimate terms with colossal amounts of effluent, it's probably best not to think about food at all.

**SUPPLIES:** However, if you do, you're sure of a warm effluent-free welcome at Tom and Wendy Thompson's The Village Shop, just south along the beach road (0.6 miles). They've also thoughtfully taken the trouble to erect a tiny clock outside in case you've forgotten to bring your time-piece with you and yet are too nervous to go into a town to consult the town-hall clock on account of your fear of large clocks (see **Phobias**, p. 78).

**PUBLIC CONVENIENCES:** A curious thing, this. You're so close to a major outflow of human waste, yet so far from anywhere public at which you might be allowed to contribute to it. The irony is almost too unbearable.

**RECOMMENDED HIDURATION:**
30–45 minutes

**DIMENSIONS:**
3m x 10m x 1.5m

**COMFORT:**
7 Plangent

**MAP REF:**
NZ 305 845

**OS LANDRANGER:** 81

## MAKINA A QUICK GETAWAY:

**TRAIN:** The area is strewn, almost to distraction, with railway lines but none of them carry anything but freight. If you are not freight, you'll have to go to Pegswood (5.5 miles) and catch a train from there.

**OTHER:** It's unlikely that there's any way of infiltrating the sewage pipe and having yourself slooshed off into the sea but that's probably just as well.

## COMPROMISED?

Try *36. Priory Corner* (38 miles).

*I am the pipe, you are the sea, as Keats might have put it.*

# 36. PRIORY CORNER

outside Lindisfarne Priory, Holy Island, Northumberland

**NEED to KNOW:** You've Aidan to thank for the fact that there's a wall here for you to duck behind. Had he not sauntered onto the island in 635 AD to build a monastery, there's every chance that nobody would have bothered doing anything here at all. Lindisfarne (aka Holy Island – so named by 11th-century monks because of the isle's ability to attract saints: Aidan, the ever-popular Cuthbert, and a whole host of martyred monks bludgeoned into beatification by Vikings) is actually an island only about half the time, since when the tide goes out, it's possible to wander out to it, much as Aidan must have done. Less violent now than when raided by those fun-loving Norse fellows in 793, an event that put a crimp in every-one's afternoon, *Priory Corner* makes the perfect retreat for those who like to feel the echoes of centuries of prayer ping about their spiritual eardrums.

**ADVANTAGES:** With a population of just 160, you can be sure that, when the tide is in, you will have only 160 people (plus any stray tourists) to avoid. This is considerably fewer than the 50 to 60 million people you might normally expect to have to steer clear of when hiding on the mainland.

**HAZARDS:** There is only one way off the island, so you may have to think out your exit strategy in advance. Some boats run from the harbour a few hundred yards away, but if you haven't brought your own, your best bet, if compromised, is to pass yourself off as the undecayed corpse of St Cuthbert.

## ESSENTIALS:

LOCAL KNOWLEDGE: The priory you are cowering behind was not built by Aidan (his entirely wooden confection has long since been eaten by marauding Vikings) but by some Benedictine monks sometime after the Norman Conquest. They had the undecayed corpse of St Cuthbert in their possession, like you did in those days if you reckoned yourself a proper cleric, and thought it might be nice if they could put him down somewhere.

**FREE FOOD:** In times past you could have counted on the monks handing out the wayfarer's dole (some bread, some beer) free of charge. Thanks to Henry VIII, you'll just have to nibble away at your own hand.

**SUPPLIES:** According to its deeply satisfying signboard, The Island Store (0.3 miles) is 'liscenced' to sell alcoholic liquors, which rather suggests the sign writer might have been paid in kind. The shop also does giftware, which is useful if you like to wear a gift from time to time.

**RECOMMENDED HIDURATION:**
30–35 minutes

**DIMENSIONS:**
3m x 3m

**COMFORT:**
6 Plebeian

**MAP REF:**
NU 127 417

**OS LANDRANGER:** 75

**PUBLIC CONVENIENCES:** By the car park at the north end of the village (0.3 miles).

**READING MATTER:** Sadly, the Lindisfarne Gospels are now at the British Library and, in any case, are too unwieldy for the serious hider to cart about. Try something by the Venerable Bede.

**COMPROMISED?** Try *39. Temple of the Muses* (36 miles).

*Lindisfarne Castle – now a sort of Edwardian country house which, despite Lutyens having been involved, is a mite disappointing.*

# HIDING IN SCOTLAND

*Scotland.*

A lot of stuff and nonsense has been written about Scotland ever since it was discovered by explorers in the late 1950s. Back then, of course, it was a land inhabited by hairy-limbed cave-dwellers dressed in nothing but dirks. A hunter-gatherer people, they preyed upon the wild haggis and the herds of bagpipes that flocked into the glens each summer to graze. These were roasted whole over open fires while the women busied themselves making the haggis into a musical instrument with which to scare the children. It was only in 1932 on the Isle of Muck that the island idiot, Numpty McKilt, during an unusually severe episode of 'the turns', cocked a snook at convention by eating the haggis and playing the bagpipes. Gradually, his fellow Muckians realised he was on to something, and before long all of Scotland had followed Numpty's lead. Although it is now universally accepted that the haggis makes for a marginally better meal than the 'pipes, no one has yet been successful in turning the latter into a musical instrument.

So much for Scottish history. What is of greater concern is whether it is a country into which one can disappear with ease into crevices and fissures.

Indeed, is it a nation wherein crevices and fissures live and move and have their being, or is it a niche-free desert like Arizona, or Derby?

The answer is hinted at in Scotland's own view of itself. Since 1992, the nose-on-a-stick-shaped nation has unofficially rebranded itself as 'The Niche Capital of the World'.[1] There is, quite naturally, a deal of blather in any claim of this sort (take, for instance, the motto 'Glasgow's Miles Better', which was apparently a shortening of the rather more factual 'Glasgow's miles better than having dental surgery performed on you by the undead'). However, in this case at least there is some foundation to the boast. One only need look at the Highlands on a bas-relief map to see that it's one of the crinkliest places on Earth. Then there are all those tiny islands (in summer, Scotland has as many as 2.25 million) biffing out of the sea then diving back in again a few hundred yards later as if they'd popped up to have a look at the non-aquatic world and, not being entirely convinced, decided to give it a miss. In some ways one can't entirely blame them, and many is the individual for whom this constitutes the principal reason for hiding. This is not, as you might first think, a bit sad but a bit happy, so think again.

Then there is the matter of population. Scots are a sociable people and tend to congregate in what are known north of the border as 'clan gatherings' – what folk beyond the confines of Scotland refer to as 'cities'. Outside of the gatherings – Glasgow, Edinburgh and Aberdeen are the names of just three, and there are others – you will find almost no one. Indeed it is a shocking fact that far fewer people choose to live in the Highlands (an area half the size of Wales) than live in Hull (an area the size of Hull). This makes it the very epitome of that old adage our grandmothers taught us: 'Where there are no people, there the hiding is good.'

Come to Scotland, then, and no one will ever know you did.[2]

[1] A claim disputed by Tibet, and even more vigorously by Dutch Guyana, although it is generally believed that this latter challenge has been made by Guyanans only to draw attention to themselves since they discovered that the rest of the world, including neighbours Brazil, doesn't quite know where the country is.

[2] If you are already in Scotland, you'll have to leave the country and then sneak back in. Bothersome, but a price worth paying.

# 37. ROBERT YOUR BRUCE

Buchan Burn, nr Glentrool Village, Kirkcudbrightshire

**NEED to KNOW:** A cosy, moss-covered rocky basin slinders peacefully under the sheltering limbs of an oak tree on the west bank of Buchan Burn. This is not just idle tittle-tattle – such a place exists and it behoves you to succumb to its embrace without delay.

**ADVANTAGES:** Views of the glen below and Buchan Hill above mean that you're unlikely to be caught unawares by evil-doers and the rancid. There is even a series of waterfalls nearby which, not unreasonably, you might have assumed you could hide behind à la *The Thirty-Nine Steps*, given that the book's author, John Buchan, shares a name with the burn over which the water tumbles. Echt an solly weil, as they say in these parts. Anyone hiding behind *these* waterfalls will soon need his brains scooping out of his boots (another local saying, apparently). However, waterfalls are known to cast health-giving negative ions into the air, so if you really are in a bit of a fix, you could always stay put and wait until all your non-ion-breathing adversaries have died of illness and disease.

**HAZARDS:** The ceaseless sip-sip-sip of water just a few feet from you may prove a nagging reminder that you should have had that operation on your dodgy heart valve before coming. Furthermore, some of the local place names sound like they might knife you in the back if they thought there was half a crown in it, to wit: Rig of the Jarkness, Neive of the Spit and Murder Hole.

## ESSENTIALS :

**LOCAL KNOWLEDGE:** Fugitive par excellence Robert the Bruce (see p. 94) won a famous propaganda victory in this glen in 1307 when, by capturing an old woman sent to spy on his forces, he was able to make a pre-emptive strike against English soldiers who were under the impression they were making a pre-emptive strike on him. Some of the biffing occurred not a stunnock's thrall from here on the banks of Loch Trool but the dead have now mostly been removed.

**FREE FOOD:** There's usually some yummy *Auricularia auricula judae* (Jew's Ear) growing on the trees hereabouts. It's brown and rubbery, and it looks like an ear, though the reason why Jewish people should wish to hear through it remains obscure.

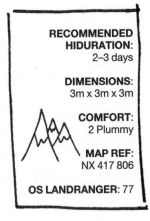

**RECOMMENDED HIDURATION:**
2–3 days

**DIMENSIONS:**
3m x 3m x 3m

**COMFORT:**
2 Plummy

**MAP REF:**
NX 417 806

**OS LANDRANGER:** 77

**SUPPLIES:** From April to autumn, the Glentrool Visitor Centre café and shop (3.5 miles). At other times, the sprawling metrovillage of Newton Stewart.

**PUBLIC CONVENIENCES:** Ditto, only more desperately so.

COMPROMISED? Try *38. Shelter of Cold Feet* (58 miles).

*Remember, in this part of Scotland a stunnock's thrall is the distance a man can heave a stone niblick, not a wooden one.*

# 38. SHELTER OF COLD FEET

**Gretna Loaning, Gretna Green, Dumfriesshire**

**NEED TO KNOW:** There are two Gretnas – Gretna and Gretna Green – and most experts agree that it's quite impossible to tell which of them is worse. As a rule of thumb, you should avoid any elopements to either if you can. However, if you should find yourself sobering up in some faux blacksmithery with not-quite-the-love-of-your-life by your side, there is still hope. First, stop talking, especially if you appear to be repeating words said to you by someone wearing some sort of imitation cassock. Without further ado, and certainly without further 'I do', turn on your heel and run, closing your ears to the cries of 'Nigel, come back' or 'But, Felicity, I love you', etc. etc. Head for the A74 and hurl yourself behind the bus shelter (here seen at night to simulate the furry sight of a newly-sobered almost-newly-wed). Lie there, breathing heavily and dazed at the extraordinary nature and/or troubled genius of your life. When a bus comes, wait until the last moment and then leap on it. Don't worry, the bus drivers are used to this and will accept payment in gold rings or, at a pinch, a really good box of confetti.

**ADVANTAGES:** A mere 200-yard dash from the Old Blacksmith's Shop, the most likely venue for your nuptious close shave.

**HAZARDS:** Jilted would-have-been brides and grooms hurling themselves in despair from the A74 flyover directly above you. It would be a sort of natural justice, I suppose, if one of them were to mash you to pulp, but messy none-theless.

**ESSENTIALS:**

LOCAL KNOWLEDGE: The Gretnas trace their major source of income back to 1754 when an act of parliament brought by Lord Harwicke made secret marriages illegal in

England and Wales. Nowadays, you have to give fifteen days' notice in Scotland so it's hardly worth the bother.

**FREE FOOD:** Unless you managed to pocket a canapé on your precipitous egress from the venue of dread, you may have to make do with grass and spiders.

**SUPPLIES:** Boutiques at the Old Blacksmith's Shop Centre (200 yards/35 seconds) will sell you whisky, 'Scotland's most unusual collection of artefacts', and things made out of Pringle.

**IF IT ALL GETS TOO MUCH:** The cash-injection-fuelled Gretna FC trample all-comers nowadays. As a result, on match days, the terraces at Raydale Park (capacity 3,000) now double as a decent alter-

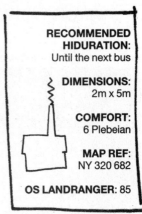

**RECOMMENDED HIDURATION:**
Until the next bus

**DIMENSIONS:**
2m x 5m

**COMFORT:**
6 Plebeian

**MAP REF:**
NY 320 682

**OS LANDRANGER:** 85

native hiding place. A 6,000 all-seater stadium for the Black and Whites is planned, at which presumably you would become doubly inconspicuous. Wear black and white. Come to think of it, you probably are already.

## MAKING A QUICK GETAWAY:

**BUS:** This will take you to one of the following places, none of which are Gretna or Gretna Green so may be considered safe: Carlisle, Moffat, Ecclefechan (beware, this may be a wholly fictional construct dreamt up to fool the English) and Lockerbie.

**COMPROMISED?** Try feigning acute amnesia or claiming that you are your own twin brother.

*If you look through the window on the extreme left you will see your jilted bride phoning her uncle. They've released him from Broadmoor now, though apparently against the advice of his psychiatrist.*

# THE HIDING SEASON

*A week spent under a weir in Nottinghamshire may not prove quite as comfortable in January as in July.*

With the onset of global warming, there is now nowhere left in Britain where one swallow does actually constitute a summer. Even Shetland, a group of islands considerably further north than Oslo,[1] still manages the odd few days when the sleet stops. This is good news, evidently, for those whose plans provide for ground-level seclusion while leaving them exposed to the mordant sky above.

Even so, it is still wise to remember that a week spent under a weir in Nottinghamshire may not prove quite as comfortable in January as in July. Then there are places such as the Cairngorm mountains above Cromarty Firth that experience all-year-round snow.[2] This conveys obvious benefits if your favourite mode of concealment is to lie down with a white sheet over yourself (for variations on this theme, see **How to be Disguised**, p. 148). However, it should also be borne in mind that where there is snow there are also penguins – birds that have been known to kill, skin and eat a man (raw) in less than an hour.

Taking these two considerations into account, we can establish that the hiding season for the common or garden hider stretches roughly from late spring to early autumn. Of course, the necessity to make oneself scarce is not always something that can be scheduled with this season in mind. This is unfortunate but there's no point in getting cross about it. Just take a deep breath, live in the moment for a bit, and recite the 'Hider's Rhyme': 'April to September, a season to remember: October to March, think about going abroad.'

[1] Not in Britain.

[2] Lest we forget, when the mountains were held by Clan Munro they were contractually obliged to supply one snowball to the King whenever he passed through.

# SCENES FROM THE
# WORLD OF SECLUSION

## nr *58. Owain's Nook*

*The secret room seen here high up in the north-west gate is widely considered the ultimate hiding place in that it can be reached only by those willing to become human cannonballs. Despite the fact that cannons are laid on (bottom left and right), there have been only three volunteers since 1856, two of whom can still be made out (middle left and right).*

# 39. TEMPLE OF THE MUSES

over the River Tweed, nr Dryburgh, Roxburghshire

**NEED to KNOW:** 'Muse /mju:z/ *Gk & Rom. Mythol.* any of the goddesses who presided over the arts and sciences.' These four – who don't appear to have been named – are credited with musing the Scottish poet James Thomson. 'Who he?' you cry. 'He of "Rule, Britannia"', the muses cry back. 'Oh dear', you cry, and rightly so. After all, waves/slaves? Come on, I think we can do better than that. To be fair, he did also write something called *The Seasons* that was a forerunner to lots of stuff by the Romantics. Anyway, what concerns us is that this memorial makes a handy temporary hiding place for those engaged in making themselves scarce along the length of the Tweed. Although the temple itself is somewhat exposed, by placing the muses strategically between yourself and any putative pursuers you can still stay satisfactorily out of view. Alternatively, join the statues as a 'Fifth Muse' in the style of Stuart Sutcliffe, the so-called Fifth Beatle. Standing perfectly still on top of a windswept hillock may not be everyone's idea of a good day out, but it's a lot less galling than deciding that your career as a painter is more worth pursuing than that as a bassist in what would become the world's biggest band *ever*, or would be had Sutcliffe lived long enough to have had the chance to regret it, which is unlikely because he really liked painting. What is more galling is that many people lazily believe he died of a drugs overdose whereas he actually suffered a cerebral haemorrhage.

**ADVANTAGES:** There's every chance that your stay here will inspire you to write that prize-winning novel about a man who dies of hypothermia because his hands freeze onto a metal statue and he can't get them loose.

**HAZARDS:** Much the same, only the novel becomes an autobiography rushed out to capitalise on your freakish death.

**LOCAL KNOWLEDGE:** Zeus and Mnemosyne had nine daughters, all of whom, by some extraordinary coincidence, went on to become muses. Calliope, Clio, Euterpe, Terpsichore, Erato, Melpomene, Thalia, Polyhymnia and Urania experienced varying degrees of success in their chosen career. Thalia became a Mexican pop star whose 1995 enormohit 'Piel Morena' is still enjoyed by bus passengers throughout Latin America on a daily basis; Terpsichore found herself immortalised in the Monty Python Cheese Shop sketch; while Calliope gave her name to a sort of steam-whistle organ favoured in the United States. Clio came off worst of all, of course, becoming a run-around car driven by someone called Nicole.

**RECOMMENDED HIDURATION:**
20–22 mins

**DIMENSIONS:**
5m diameter

**COMFORT:**
3 Pleasant

**MAP REF:**
NT 588 322

**OS LANDRANGER:**
73/74

**FREE FOOD:** Food for thought.

**SUPPLIES:** The Dryburgh Abbey shop (0.3 miles), aside from stocking all the staples of hiding life such as fudge, clan ties and fridge magnets, also does an excellent line in gargoyles.

**PUBLIC CONVENIENCES:** Also at Dryburgh Abbey (0.3 miles) though, depending on how well acquainted you are with the moral high ground, you might feel obliged to purchase a gargoyle or two on every visit.

**URBAN MYTH:** Queen Victoria famously said: 'We are not a muse.'

**COMPROMISED?** Try *40. Welcome to Glasgow* (64 miles).

*In Scotland, sculptors are wont to charge extra for eyes with pupils.*

# 40. WELCOME to GLASGOW

under the old railway, corner of Nelson Street and Bridge Street, Glasgow

**NEED to KNOW:** Glasgow – it's not what you think, you know. This hiding place is no longer indicative of the city at all. Glasgow nowadays is a place of rolling fields interrupted only very occasionally by a building here or there (for one must have art galleries). These colonnaded temples to the painted canvas (if you're looking for video installations masquerading as art, you'll have to go to Edinburgh) also act as portals to the underground world in which all Glaswegians live in order not to mess up the view 'above stairs' as they call it. This hiding place under the old railway, nominally at the point where Bridge Street and Nelson Street once met, is the last ugly place in Glasgow and was kept from the bulldozers only by dint of a campaign by local historians who wished future generations to know something of the city's past.

**ADVANTAGES:** Hurry along now and you may still find the abandoned suitcase here. Climb into it and you create the Holy Grail of Hiding – the hiding place within a hiding place. Of course, any holy grail that can merely be created isn't really up to much, but don't bother writing to *Hiding Monthly* – they refuse to publish any letters on the subject. I think it's because the editor's grandfather was once married to one of the Mitfords.

**HAZARDS:** When Glasgow was a conventional overground city, the people there suffered from a variety of illnesses brought on by the unhealthy urban environment. Not wishing to burden their overstretched GPs with their ailments, most Glaswegians would self-medicate. This is why you will find a large number of syringes scattered around among the carefully preserved lager cans and plastic bags.

Even if you have an ailment, it's probably best not to use any of these syringes without first washing them very thoroughly.

## ESSENTIALS:

**LOCAL KNOWLEDGE:** St Mungo is revered in Glasgow, and his church (one of such beauty that it was allowed to stand during the ruralisation of the city) is well worth a visit. St Mary's is a picturesque ruin in perfect picnic country. However, the church named in honour of St Midge has sadly been lost.

**FREE FOOD:** Rats roam here freely, having been driven out of most of the city as a result of the re-introduction of indigenous mammals such as otters and stoats.

**RECOMMENDED HIDURATION:**
2–4 hours

**DIMENSIONS:**
1m x 10m x 3m

**COMFORT:**
9 Playful

**MAP REF:**
NS 586 644

**OS LANDRANGER:** 64

**SUPPLIES:** At one time you might have frequented The Lunch Box and the Norfolk News and Convenience Store just a half-brick's throw away in Norfolk Street. Now you'll just have to live on nuts and berries like the rest of the population.

**PUBLIC CONVENIENCES:** Nobody minds nowadays if you just find a tree.

COMPROMISED? Try 37. *Robert Your Bruce* (53 miles).

*Glasgow of Yesteryear. Where these buses ran, now only a lazy brook meanders through a forest glade. The Glaswegian pub on the corner has become a wooded hillock from which, on a clear day, you can see the Western Isles.*

# KING CHARLES II
## (1630–85)

Hiduration: 42 days
Value as role model: 9/10

'Mind yourself on that twig,
Your Highness.'

Historians disagree among themselves, but you can take it as read
that those were the very words
used over 350 years ago by Colonel
Carlis to warn the future Charles II of
imminent arboreal unpleasantness.
'Verily, if the oak twig bites', quipped the royal-personage-in-waiting in
reply, 'I shall hang it for a treasonable fellow. Get it, Carlis? Tree-sonable. By
Harry, I'm good.'

So began one of the best-known hiding stories in British history, and
one that over 500 Royal Oak pubs bear testament to today. What is less well
known is that the oak tree played but a cameo role in a bravura hiding
performance that gives the lie to the commonly held belief that all the royals
since Good Queen Bess have been a bit namby-pamby.

By 3 September 1651 the game was well and truly up for Charles Stuart,
a king in name alone. He was a stripling 21-year-old; both parts of his father
had been cold in the grave for nearly three years; his army had just been
irretrievably routed at Worcester; and if he were to fall into the hands of the
Roundheads all he had to look forward to was a summary trial followed by
execution.

Keen not to become a chip off the old block in more than one sense,
Charles fled from Worcester with a tiny entourage and passed through
Stourbridge to arrive at dawn at Whiteladies, the house of one George
Penderel. Here he took on the identity of a humble hedge-mender, donning
'a coarse noggen shirt … breeches of green coarse cloth, and a doeskin,
leather doublet'. Although a royal fugitive today might be ill-advised to wear
too much noggen, even while travelling in the countryside, in 17th-century
Britain it was the material of choice for the billhook-wielding masses.

However, Charles' adoption of a 'long, white steeple-crowned hat' does suggest that he had still not entirely lost his taste for the theatrical. Crucially, he was taught to mimic the accent of the local working man (there was only one, apparently, and he kindly agreed to teach His Highness) and tutored in the arts of the peasant's trademark feckless shamble.

From here Charles attempted to reach Wales – in the main, a hopelessly royalist sort of place – but had to turn back on finding the bridges over the Severn closely guarded. After a night in a barn he was back at Whiteladies, from where he made the short journey to Boscobel House, arriving cold and wet and with his feet cut to ribbons. It was in the nearby wood that Charles and Colonel Carlis spent their memorable day in the oak while roundhead soldiers prowled around below.

By this time a £1,000 reward had been offered for information leading to the capture of the 'malicious and dangerous traitor'. Charles spent an understandably uncomfortable night in a priest hole intended for a priest shorter than he was.

In the morning he rubbed some feeling back into his legs and headed for Moseley Hall, while soldiers pounced on Whiteladies and Boscobel. When the Parliamentarian troops called at Moseley, the owner Thomas Whitgreave went out to meet them and successfully feigned being too ill to countenance harbouring royal fugitives.

Believing it was time to move on, Charles travelled that night to Bentley Hall where he became William Jackson, a tenant farmer and manservant to Colonel Lane's daughter Jane. On their way to Long Marston, near Stratford-upon-Avon, the horse that 'Jackson' and Jane were riding inopportunely lost a shoe. As the servant, Charles had to deal with the blacksmith. Quite the actor, he apparently played the part to perfection, telling the man that 'if that rogue [i.e. he himself] were taken, he deserved to be hanged'.

Things almost went belly-up at Long Marston when Charles admitted he didn't know how to wind a machine used for turning a spit. The cook became suspicious. Thinking on his feet, he claimed that his family were so poor they rarely had meat and when they did so, they turned the spit by hand.

The wanderings continued – first to Cirencester, then Abbots Leigh, via Bristol. Not finding a suitable boat there to take Charles to France, the royal party went back across country to Castle Cary and on to the Wyndham family in Trent, a village on the Somerset/Dorset border. A fellow named Limbry was sailing the following week to St-Malo and agreed to pick up Charles at Charmouth under cover of darkness.

The King then became manservant to his fellow fugitive Henry Wilmot, the Earl of Rochester, who was posing as a would-be groom eloping with a cousin of the Wyndhams, like you do. They took lodgings at Charmouth to await the boat. The fateful night came and they squatted on the beach until daybreak, but the boat failed to materialise. They assumed that some treachery was afoot. In fact, the boatman's wife had wormed out of him what he was doing and had locked him in their bedroom in terror that he would be caught and executed.

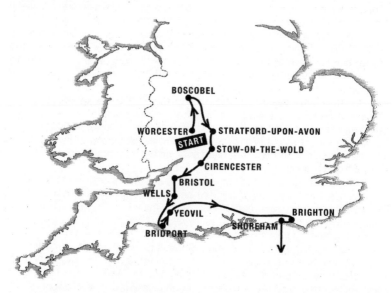

Charles fled to Bridport, only to find it unhelpfully full of Parliamentarian soldiers about to be shipped to Jersey. When an ostler there claimed in a loud voice that he recognised Charles' face from somewhere, the monarch managed to persuade him that they had met years before when both were with the same employer. The shaves were getting closer.

Meanwhile, Wilmot (the would-be groom – do keep up) had *his* horse shed a shoe. The blacksmith he went to happened to be a Roundhead soldier who noticed that the other three shoes were made in three different counties, all of which Charles himself had had cause to visit. The super-sleuth informed his commanding officer, who dashed to Bridport, missing Charles by minutes. The royal band had trooped off into the country and got themselves thoroughly lost, arriving eventually at the village of Broadwindsor where they took refuge at an inn, only to be joined later by billeted Roundhead soldiers.

In despair, Charles returned to Trent, where he lay low for nearly three weeks while Wilmot tried to arrange a boat. Eventually, a Nicholas Tettersell from Brighthelmstone (later Brighton) was engaged for the appropriately princely sum of £110. Charles sneaked over to Heale House near Salisbury, and then to Hambledon where, to deceive a drunk and suspicious guest, he had to pretend to be Roundhead. The next day there was another lengthy horse-ride to Brighthelmstone via Houghton and Bramber. At Beeding a drunk landlord (most of England was drunk most of the time by this stage, but that's what civil wars do to you) recognised Charles but, being a Royalist, didn't give him away. Tettersell winkled a cool £200 insurance out of Charles's protectors before allowing Charles on board *Surprise* and sailing from Shoreham at high tide the following morning. A mere two hours later, Roundhead soldiers poured into the harbour on a tip-off.

There was still time for one last deception – *Surprise* made as if for the Isle of Wight until it was out of sight from the shore, when it abruptly changed course for Fécamp, a tiny French harbour. Privateers (that's pirates to you and me) from Ostend appeared out of nowhere and Charles had to persuade Tettersell to let him and Wilmot off on a cock-boat, whatever that is. It was left to a Quaker called Richard Carver to carry Charles from the boat onto French soil (well, sand) and safety.

> **Lesson:** Even if you are a bit posh, you should still find it within you to evade an entire army for six weeks and get clean away to France in order to wait for a republic to fall so you can come back and repay everyone's faith in you by being a bit of a useless king.

# 41. BAILIE FYFE'S CLOSE

**Bailie Fyfe's Close, 107 High Street, Edinburgh, Midlothian**

**NEED TO KNOW:** Had we but world enough, and time – as tip-top poet and politician Andrew Marvell (1621–78) was wont to quoth – we'd probably spend a good deal of it skulking around behind gritty staircases. This one is conveniently positioned on the Royal Mile and is within spectacularly easy reach – even for those with tinier hands than those mused upon by tip-top poet and typographist e.e. cummings (1894–1962) – of more kilts and sick animal dispensing than you can shake a stick of Edinburgh rock at. This is clearly a hiding place for bons viveurs who like the occasional dash of asceticism in their *cocktail de vie*. Admittedly, the occupant has barely room to swing a cat, but this is probably just as well because anyone attempting same would have the folk from the PDSA next door down on them like a ton of ducks. Good thing too, in my opinion.

**ADVANTAGES:** The rough ground behind Bailie Fyfe's Close should prove large enough a tract for even the most mediocre of helicopter pilots to land on. And which of us, if we scrabbled through our old address books, could not alight upon the name of some friend or acquaintance who, though an appallingly bad helicopter pilot, could nevertheless be counted upon to rescue us from imminent detection at a moment's notice?

**HAZARDS:** As may be perceived from the photograph above, this staircase has long since relocated from the world of the purely functional to that of the outrageously aesthetic. You should therefore be mindful that the piece could attract aesthetes. The best thing to do if discovered by such a one as these is to stay calm and appear to be part of an installation. If you learn a few words of Czech and repeat them in a dull monotone, backwards, the illusion is complete. Be warned, though: if you become proficient enough, and your hcezC makes sly allusions to political figures from the Eastern Bloc of the 1970s, you could find yourself in the running for a Fringe award which could make you a little more conspicuous than is ideal.

## ESSENTIALS :

**LOCAL KNOWLEDGE:** This close has been around since 1572 but assumed its present name as recently as 1686 when named after the magistrate ('bailie') Gilbert Fyfe. Two centuries later a tenement here collapsed, putting an end to 35 of its inhabitants. Mourn ye.

**RECOMMENDED HIDURATION:**
2–4 hours

**DIMENSIONS:**
1.5m x 6m

**COMFORT:**
2 Plummy

**MAP REF:**
NT 260 737

**OS LANDRANGER:** 66

**SUPPLIES:** A variety of establishments on the Royal Mile exist only to meet your exacting gastronomic exigencies. Many also do take-aways, presumably to minimise the amount of time the city's hiders spend alfresco (little knowing that you yourself are pretty darn alfresco even in hiding).

**URBAN MYTH:** The Turkish language possesses a single word for the taking of a group photograph by a waiter.

## COMPROMISED? Try 40. Welcome to Glasgow (42 miles).

*The fabled jar of King David I is said to have rendered fleeing Jacobites invisible for over 200 years.*

137

# 42. A CROWN OF HORNS

Glen Forsa, Isle of Mull, Inner Hebrides, Argyllshire

**NEED TO KNOW:** Few people, when considering the manner of their own death, care to spend much time contemplating the possibility that it might involve a good goring by Highland cattle before being hung out to dry on a gorse bush. The conditions at *A Crown of Horns* are therefore highly favourable, since there is much to dissuade would-be seekers from taking too keen an interest in the place: first off, there is a convenient gorse bush to nip behind and, secondly, an abundance of Highlandness roams the valley in search of human flesh. The fact that the hairful hornèd ones are cows rather than bulls mattereth little, since most folk, already wary on account of the gibbetine gorse bushes, are unlikely to stay around long enough to discern the difference.

**ADVANTAGES:** Gorse. Floppy fringes. Fresh air. A steady supply of plankton (see below).

**HAZARDS:** Since, grammatically speaking, clothes are 'hung' while people are 'hanged', is a person 'hung up to dry' or 'hanged up to dry'? It's a pedant's nightmare.

## ESSENTIALS:

**LOCAL KNOWLEDGE:** Glen Forsa is, needless to say, the Norse for 'glen of the swiftly flowing river'. Most Norse words appear to mean something along these lines – 'steep hill near the sea', 'small village amongst farmsteads', that sort of thing. All that detailed juxtaposition within single words makes one suspect that most conversations carried out between Norsefolk were rather laborious affairs. Even a simple shopping trip to buy the ingredients for a birthday cake would be something of an arduous enterprise. CUSTOMER: Frona, pelpin, Gutssonknutsson. ('The flour amidst the shelving, if it is to your pleasing, son-of-Gut-son-of-Knut.') SHOP ASSISTANT: Fronheta kin frongleta? ('The wholemeal flour borne from a hundred wheat fields, or

the plain flour amidst the softly melting cheese?')
CUSTOMER: Na, fronkelpstinan. ('No, the self-raising
flour adjoining the pie fillings that taste of kelp.')
SHOP ASSISTANT: Greppel, medem. ('I'm afraid we're
all out of that, madam'.) CUSTOMER: Pasht. Pogrig.
('Oh, forget it then. I'll buy a cake.') SHOP ASSISTANT:
Pogrugiga kin pogregiga? ('The cake made in the
kitchen by the winding stream, or the cake baked in
the oven above the caves that resemble the mouths
of giants?') Etc., etc.

**FREE FOOD:** The cheery Gulf Stream warms the
sea around Mull, making it rich in plankton. For a
tasty meal, swim around for a bit under water with
your mouth open.

**RECOMMENDED HIDURATION:**
6–8 hours

**DIMENSIONS:**
2m x 2m

**COMFORT:**
3 Pleasant

**MAP REF:**
NM 609 390

**OS LANDRANGER:** 49

**SUPPLIES:** A supermarket in miniature at Craignure
(7 miles) caters for all your nutritional needs that cannot be met by plankton alone,
while second-hand clothing and old board games that turn out to be not so much fun
as you'd remembered them can be purchased very close by at the charity shop Island
Castaways (full marks for the name there, boys and girls).

**PUBLIC CONVENIENCES:** Fine examples opposite the Craignure ferry terminal.

**MAKING A QUICK GETAWAY:**

**TRAIN:** That old hiders' favourite, the narrow gauge railway, conveys the flee-ee all
the way from Craignure to Torosay Castle (and Gardens), a distance of no less than a
mile (Adult Single £3, special deals on combined Rail/Castle/Gardens tickets).

**COMPROMISED?** Try 43. At Home with Clan Destine (31 miles).

'My cow's got no eyes.' 'How does he smell?' *No. Hang on, that's not right.*

139

# WHAT SORT OF HIDER ARE YOU?

It was philosopher and dandy Stuart Goddard who declared, 'Even though you fool your soul / Your conscience will be mine',[1] and it cannot be argued but that time has proved him right. It is regrettable then that many people feel that fooling their souls is still a viable option when they come to don their favourite hiding garb and disappear into the mist. If you are such a person – and if you are over 35 it's statistically likely that you are – the sooner you disabuse yourself of this canard, the better.

Start off by taking as read the fact that every hider falls into one of the following categories. If you bleat that you fit into none of them, you are not only fooling your soul but yourself too, which in many ways is worse. Wilful self-delusion is, after all, the beginning of a Monopoly game in which you are the only player: it may feel good when you win but your hotels will be empty.

**The Dissembler**
A man or woman more than usually eager to befuddle the opposition. The opposition in such cases tends to include the rest of the world, so hiding from everyone is often the easiest way the Dissembler has of disguising his or her motives, which are more shocking than the world could possibly imagine and at which even the most salacious of newspaper editors might pale. Hiding is probably the best service the Dissembler can do humankind and on no account should any attempt be made to find such a person.

**The Weekender**
Typically a man, the Weekender hides from Friday evening to Sunday evening and most Bank Holidays in search of what he calls 'cave time'. In reality, he would like to hide for good but finds himself ensnared by his actuarial job

[1] (All mine)

into spending his weekdays in an office assessing the risks taken by others that he himself cannot bring himself to take. The irony is so affecting that he is frequently found by colleagues with his head inside the office microwave which he has unplugged in the mistaken belief that this will work in the same way as an unlit gas oven. Tears. Premiums. Bedtime.

### The Crier for Help
What yelps in yonder quarry? It is the Crier for Help, hiding while all the time yearning to be found.[2] Ironically, often very successful hiders in that they opt for hiding places so obvious that no one bothers to search for them there. This can sometimes lead to the regrettable circumstance in which the Crier for Help is forced to jump about waving his or her arms, wailing: 'Look at me, I'm hidden.'

[2] See also **Agatha Christie** (p. 38).

## The Athlete

Habitually hides while clothed in a tracksuit and, if really serious, one of those nose clips that splays the nostrils and makes the wearer appear as if they are about to carry out a frenzied attack on a picador. (Of which, bull fighting? What's *that* all about?) Chooses hiding places according to the physical exertion required to get to them. Indeed, Athletes prefer to be 'on the run' rather than hiding in one place. It is because of this that they often find themselves barred from membership of the more 'purist' local branches of the Hiding Association.[3]

## The I-Didn't-Choose-To-Be-Born

Those for whom the act of hiding essentially represents an eternally doomed quest to return to the womb.

[3] The Hiding Association (founded 1965) is Britain's only mass membership organisation dedicated to the advancement of hiding. Looked down upon by more secretive hiding groups for having once accidentally published the address of its head office, the association has nonetheless remained successfully hidden since 1986 and is the only national organisation to be on the Metropolitan Police Missing Persons List. Currently rumoured to be run from the bottom of a lake in Staffordshire.

# SCENES FROM THE WORLD OF SECLUSION

## nr *60. Ynys Gifftan*

*By 400 BC the Celts had developed five uses for sand but still had no word to describe a sitcom in which each of the characters represents a common personality type.*

# 43. AT HOME WITH CLAN DESTINE

**Coire Gabhail, Glen Coe, Argyllshire**

**NEED to KNOW :** Coire Gabhail, a hidden valley high up on the southern side of Glen Coe, would probably be of little interest to anyone but geography teachers if it were not for the fact that Clan Donald, who inhabited the glen, were in the habit of using the valley to stash the livestock they had spirited away from their good friends the Campbells, the MacGregors, the Stewarts, the Camerons, the Mackintoshes, and indeed anyone else whose cattle and chattels they could plunder. Before you get the wrong idea though, all the clans were up to it. For centuries on end, the Highlands were like some mad children's game where each group has to steal balloons off every other group until a small girl trips over her party frock and hits her head against the arm of a sofa.

**ADVANTAGES :** A fine example of double-hiddenness – first by the valley itself and then by this cave made by a huge boulder. Furthermore, the entrance to Coire Gabhail is famously narrow enough to be blocked by a single tree trunk or three-quarters of a ton of sugared mice.

**HAZARDS :** Many of Clan Donald managed to escape the massacre of Glen Coe (of which, more later) by fleeing in their bedclothes through a blizzard and hiding in Coire Gabhail. Although this was evidently preferable to being shot, sliced or burnt, some did not survive the night. It might therefore be an idea to don more than your usual nightwear while here, even if you plan to hide only during the hours of daylight.

**LOCAL KNOWLEDGE:** The English have done many bad things in their time. However, if you are English, there's no need to go into particular paroxysms of angst over the massacre that occurred here in 1692 (the same year as the Salem Witch Trials, for which the English were arguably more responsible, if only by descent). Contrary to popular belief, the slaughter was orchestrated by a Scotsman (Sir John Dalrymple, the Master of Stair), based on an original idea by another Scot (Sir John Campbell of Glenorchy), ordered by a Dutchman (King William III), and carried out by Campbell soldiers. Can't get us there.

**FREE FOOD:** There are no stolen cattle here now, and even if there were, it would probably be a mistake to eat them, all things considered.

**RECOMMENDED HIDURATION:**
6–8 weeks

**DIMENSIONS:**
3m x 2m x 2m

**COMFORT:**
2 Plummy

**MAP REF:**
NN 171 560

**OS LANDRANGER:** 41

**SUPPLIES:** A perfectly adequate shop in Glencoe (5 miles) opens later than you might think, but don't arrive much later than you might think, because it will be closed by then.

**PUBLIC CONVENIENCES:** In the village of Glencoe which, handily, is just one word so you know you're referring to *that* rather than the *glen* of Glen Coe. Except, of course, if you're speaking you have to say the village's name quite fast while leaving a bit of a pause in between the two words of the glen, or the distinction is lost. Local schoolchildren learn the habit by being made to repeat 'Glenn Close' and 'Glucose' until such time as they pass out.

**COMPROMISED?** Try *44. Behind the Goals* (54 miles).

*Coire Gabhail – a valley so hidden that this photo of it may not even exist.*

# 44. BEHIND THE GOALS

**Memorial Park, Blair Atholl, Perthshire**

**NEED TO KNOW:** To resourceful hiders, even an unassuming park in a small village can offer up fertile pastures wherein they may reap where they have not sown. In this case, the Memorial Park is the architect of its own fecundity, sprouting a five-a-side-football-cum-tennis-court with transepts that both accommodate the goal posts (these being very popular in the Scottish form of tennis) and provide sheltered spaces outside the court-cum-pitch in which a man or a woman may crouch down (see **How to Crouch**, p. 64).

**ADVANTAGES:** The location gives, if not a grandstand view, at least a croucher's eye view of 'Fortress Memorial', as Blair Atholl Star FC's home ground is doubtless known to their adversaries in the Perthshire Amateur League. Despite winning both the Division 3 Championship and the North Perthshire Cup in the 2005/06 season, their crowds barely outnumber the young hopefuls warming the subs' bench, so you may watch without any real fear of detection.

**HAZARDS:** By the law of averages or physics or something, at some point it simply has to stop raining here. Indubitably, when it does so the grateful locals rush out of their homes in their tennis whites, drain the court, and dish up the kind of tennisial spectacle that would grace Roland Garros if only the French Tennis Association had the foresight to install goal posts. Inevitably, at some juncture in the game, a stray ball is bound to fly out and land somewhere near your crouching person, which could be potentially awkward. Also, the only private army in Europe, the Atholl Highlanders, is stationed across the road at Blair Castle, which is enough to make even the coolest of hiders a little uneasy.

**LOCAL KNOWLEDGE:** As anyone who has landed even the most glancing of blows at Shakespearean tragedy will tell you, Birnam Wood (currently just 18 miles away from Blair Atholl) is one of those rare shifty plantations that cannot be counted on to remain in the same place for any reasonable length of time. Last seen at Dunsinane, it could turn up more or less anywhere in central Scotland. However, it has now been reduced to a single tree – the Birnam Oak – so you should remain calm but watchful.

**FREE FOOD:** Daffodils. That's it. Cheer up, there are many ways of serving them.

**RECOMMENDED HIDURATION:**
2–3 hours

**DIMENSIONS:**
2m x 2m

**COMFORT:**
6 Plebeian

**MAP REF:**
NN 873 653

**OS LANDRANGER:** 43

**SUPPLIES:** The post office (0.1 miles) comes garlanded with the many cups and shields won by the village's pipe bands. If you believe that music is its own reward, there is also Atholl Stores just around the corner, with whose entirely untrophied window you might find yourself more in tune, so to speak.

**PUBLIC CONVENIENCES:** The Memorial Park has its own (80 yards), as befits a fortress.

**TRAIN:** *Behind the Goals* is right next door to the station, from where the occasional train will convey you to villages that have been lost for hundreds of years.

Try *48. The Benches of Hard Knocks* (70 miles).

*This is why Spot-the-Ball is such a lottery. Blair Atholl Star under the cosh but nervelessly holding out against First Division Stanley FC in the first round of the Consolation Cup.*[1]

[1] Final score, because you cannot help yourself from wanting to know:
Blair Atholl Star (0) 0 v 2 (0) Stanley.

# HOW TO BE DISGUISED

Many experienced hiders like to employ a disguise to and from their chosen hiding places, and it's an option you should consider if there is any danger at all of you being rumbled en route. After all, there's nothing so frustrating as being found even before you've started to hide. A good disguise also means that the long-term hider, rather than having to remain permanently out of eyeshot in some miserable hovel in the mountains, can mingle freely in society from time to time without his or her true identity being unveiled.

That said, it should be stated straight away that the world of not being who you really are contains many pitfalls, not the least of which is the fatal blurring at the point where disguise becomes fancy dress. You may think that staying quiet in some corner seat of a train wearing a Pierrot costume is sufficient for your fellow passengers to take you for a just another harmless mime artist on his way to the opening of an art gallery. However, if this were the case, art galleries would be opening all the time and the figures quite clearly show that this is not so.

The key to good disguise, then, is to blend in with your surroundings. For instance, your Highland Warrior outfit, though spectacularly successful in the mountains above Aviemore, is likely to prove a liability on the streets of Weymouth. Therefore, give some thought to the milieu into which you are hoping to merge. To start you off, here are some handy tips on simple accessories you can add to your ordinary clothes or face in order to mix inconspicuously with the locals in various parts of the country without stooping to the lazy mimicry of regional stereotyping.

Glasgow: a tam-o'-shanter (worn jauntily, except on Sundays)
Cardiff: (to 2007) a badge in the shape of the FA Cup
Newcastle: clogs
Birmingham: an expression of ineffable sadness
East Anglia: straw

(Also note: No one in London speaks English as a first language, so do be sure to pick up an accent and some grammatical idiosyncrasies before passing through.)

Of course, the right disguise for one person might be a complete no-go area for another. The expert hider knows the difference; the amateur merely flaps in the direction of the difference, as if fearful of an oncoming forward. It is eminently preferable therefore to decide what works for you *before* circumstances overrun you, as they surely will if you continue on the dissolute course you have chosen for yourself hitherto. Sloppiness is not an option, even in these days of 'smart casual' and the airbag.

Consider then the following disguisal accoutrements and make a mental tick or cross against each one:

- [ ] Hat (whether bowler, pork pie, wimple)
- [ ] False hair (beard, moustache, wig, ear fuzz)
- [ ] Glasses (NHS, early-career Elton John, dark, Guinness)
- [ ] Pipe (meerschaum, churchwarden, hose)

If you remember nothing else, remember this: adopting a disguise is not just dressing up, it's about taking on a whole other identity. You should therefore think about your character's back story – has he or she ever done a stretch for the attempted theft of Belgium, for instance? My personal favourite persona is that of 'Havill', the under-butler whose high cheek bones and aquiline nose have caused havoc below stairs at more than one country house in Hertfordshire (for more of his exploits, see **How to Crouch**, p. 64). You, of course, must choose your own path. Your ability to become that path may well determine your chances of arriving at your selected hiding place free from the ignominy of being uncovered, unmasked, debunked and stoned in front of a vast baying mob of indignant people you once considered friends. So it's probably worth your while getting in some practice at home first.

# 45. Hmmm

Isle of Bìoruaslum, off Vatersay/Bhatarsaigh, off Barra, Outer Hebrides, Ross-shire

**NEED TO KNOW:** An obscure island off an obscure island off the southernmost inhabited island in the remotest chain of islands off the west coast of Scotland, *Hmmm* is likely to appeal to the already friendless and Vatersayans alike, the latter no doubt pleased to discover that, if nothing else, at least they have a hiding place on their doorstep.

**ADVANTAGES:** The corncrake, a bird misused for centuries by poets hungry for a rhyme for 'cornflake', is now but a rare thing. However, its distinctive 'crex crex' can occasionally be heard in the early morning or late evening by the rocks and stones of Bìoruaslum. For indeed, these are magic rocks and stones that can hear and smell and, some locals aver, even taste. The corncrake too can be said to be uncommonly gifted in that it speaks in the tongue of ancient Rome, although admittedly its vocabulary extends only as far as *Crex crex*, its Latin name, which doesn't make for much of a conversation. Still, it's fun to ask one what its Latin name is and hear it give the correct answer. None of this is of much benefit in making the hiding place any more secure but it does help pass the time.

**HAZARDS:** It's not an easy island to get on to, and the sheep wandering in blissful frequlence over Vatersay are wont to snigger at your rather baleful attempts to do so. It does a person no good to be sniggered at by a sheep, and nothing can quite prepare one for it.

**ESSENTIALS:**

**LOCAL KNOWLEDGE:** Just around the corner from here, at Cornaig Bay, there was a stone (since lost to the sea) at which large numbers of beheadings were conducted during the reign of 'Marion of the Heads'. Apparently, she kicked the whole thing off in 1427 by having her stepsons decapitated, and enjoyed it so much that she continued in like manner with the locals. The practice has since been discontinued, almost entirely, so you've little cause to worry.

**FREE FOOD:** Flotsam and jetsam mainly. An old Hebridean saying implies that any flotsam beached before dawn will taste of curry if eaten with the sea still fresh on it, but there is little evidence to suggest that this is true.

**SUPPLIES:** There are no shops on Bioruaslum. There is no longer a shop on Vatersay either, though there is a tiny post office in a sort of shed in someone's garden in the main village. This is all well and good if you require a television licence or an E111 form, but these are of negligible nutritional value (unless eaten with the sea fresh on them) so you would be better off hauling yourself over to Castlebay (3.5 miles) on Barra, where two grocers and a superishmarket vie for your custom like corncrakes attempting to discuss the finer points of the Middle East crisis but able to do so only by the use of subtly differing inflections of their own name in Latin. It's a joy to watch.

**PUBLIC CONVENIENCES:** Not really an Outer Hebs thing.

COMPROMISED? Try *42. A Crown of Horns* (75 miles).

**RECOMMENDED HIDURATION:**
2–3 weeks

**DIMENSIONS:**
500m x 400m

**COMFORT:**
2 Plummy

**MAP REF:**
NL 611 963

**OS LANDRANGER:** 31

*The sea, empty of all but the sound of a certain bird painfully constructing his argument in which the recognition of Palestine as a nation state is a vital prelude to long-lasting peace.*

# 46. THE SECRET GATE

Mitchell Hill Cemetery, Dingwall/Inbhir Pheofharain, Ross and Cromarty

## NEED TO KNOW:

Don't be put off by the fact that this corner of a Scottish field is groaning under the weight of symbolism, to wit: a secret gate, embraced by an evergreen, leading from a cemetery (or is it *to* a cemetery?). Even Freud admits that sometimes a cigar is just a cigar. Perhaps your desire to hide here merely stems from a fondness for the central Highlands and has nothing to do with your subconscious yearning to rush headlong into the arms of the eternal, thereby escaping death.

## ADVANTAGES:

Actually being here and seeing the gate, the tree and the cemetery for what they are and not for the potent subliminal tale they would appear to tell is oddly comforting. What is more, the tree and its neighbour give ample protection not only from the rain but the rain of despair that is the inevitable consequence of childhood's clouds of longing.

## HAZARDS:

Often misconstrued as the mere singular of a happening London music venue, Dingwall is, nevertheless, a town fierce with meaning and should not necessarily be seen as a place of refuge if the coded significance of *The Secret Gate* becomes too heavy a weight for your shoulders to bear.

## ESSENTIALS:

**LOCAL KNOWLEDGE:** The loose collection of letters that passes for Dingwall's Gaelic name (see above) literally means 'great warrior brought low by a spiteful letter in a colonial newspaper', so it is apt that the mighty tower in the grounds of the cemetery is dedicated to the memory of the tragic Major-General Sir Hector Archibald MacDonald (1853–1903). A war hero (all right, a hero to expansionist Britannia, perhaps not so well loved by those batting for the other sides), he was the subject of a spiteful letter in the *Times of Ceylon* that spread the (almost certainly baseless) rumour that 'he does not like ladies' (he was, after all, happily married). Coming down to breakfast at the Hotel Regina in Paris, he discovered that the charges of immorality had become headline news. He went back to his room and promptly shot himself. There have since been rumours (probably also baseless) that in fact the old soldier faked his own death and went on to become Commander-in-Chief of the German forces on the Eastern Front. Not your everyday conventional icon, then.

**FREE FOOD**: What is food but the temporary satisfaction of the oral fixation?

**SUPPLIES**: Dingwall's pedestrian High Street (0.5 miles) is jam-packed with jam, and packages of things that aren't jam but which might go well with it – you just have to buy the package and hope: it's the Dingwall way. If you open the package and find you've splashed out, not on crumpets or scones as anticipated, but a Junior Boxing Set with Real Punch-Ball or a contract to re-lay parts of the A51, you'll just have to eat the jam straight out of the jar, though hopefully not in the same quantities as those folk on VE Day who over-indulged and promptly died of sugar poisoning.

**PUBLIC CONVENIENCES**: Secreted in the car park at the foot of the hill but worth the seeking out (0.4 miles).

COMPROMISED? Try *47. Keith!* (55 miles).

> **RECOMMENDED HIDURATION:**
> 5–7 days
>
> **DIMENSIONS**:
> 5m x 4m x 2m
>
> **COMFORT**:
> 1 Plush
>
> **MAP REF**:
> NH 549 583
>
> **OS LANDRANGER**: 26

*Symbol, symbol, symbol, symbol, symbol, symbol, symbol, symbol.*

# LAWRENCE OF ARABIA
## (1888–1935)

> **Hiduration:** 13 years, on and off
> **Value as role model:** 7/10

Polyglot, spy, cartographer, uniter of disparate Arab peoples, legend. I'm sure your biographer will probably describe you in similar terms (although one would hope that the opening sentence of the story of *your* life might contain a main verb). However, what made Thomas Edward Lawrence different from you was his almost mythic ability to hide himself in early life and his totally wretched and abject attempts to repeat the performance once he'd passed 30. You, if I recall correctly, have done much the reverse and now look back on those early years with something approaching embarrassment.

The younger Lawrence was indeed brilliant at concealing himself and/or his true identity when he really needed to. Since very often 'when he really needed to' tended to encompass those times when, if captured, he would have been parted from his gizzards one giblet at a time and had his head sent to Constantinople to be used as a ceremonial spittoon, it's probably just as well he was.[1]

Take the occasion, for example, when Lawrence was in Hejaz on a mission to glean information about Arab forces. Wearing a khaki uniform and a *qalifeh*, he was naturally mistaken by the Arabs for a Syrian deserter from the Turkish army. Thus, when he casually drilled them for information, he

---

[1] To be fair to Turkish soldiery, on the one occasion Lawrence did allegedly fall into their hands – at Dera in November 1917 – he claimed that he was merely interrogated, manhandled, whipped and gang-raped before managing to escape. However, there are grave doubts as to whether this episode actually took place at all, so it's quite possible that the Turks have been maligned all these years. On the credit side, it is a compliment to be thought of as a 'Young Turk', which must be some consolation to those living in the would-be European nation.

lent a Syrian accent to his perfect Arabic. Then of course there was all the running around attacking trains and blowing up railway lines he so enjoyed. Such guerrilla operations obliged him to nip back repeatedly into the desert where he and his comrades melted effortlessly into their surroundings. So far so good.

However, compare and contrast this with the stabs at achieving anonymity by the now world-famous Lawrence of Arabia. He enlisted in the RAF in August 1922 as an ordinary ranker named John Hume Ross.[2] This cover lasted for the few hours it took the RAF to check the name with Somerset House. Still, strings were pulled and he was allowed to join up. However, so lacklustre was the disguise of his real identity that just four months later an officer tipped off the *Daily Express* and the cat was not just out of the bag but throwing up fur balls all over the lawn.

Lawrence had another go in March 1923, this time signing up with the Royal Tank Corps as a T.E. Shaw. Err, hello? *T.E.*? Is there some sort of clue there, Thomas Edward? Predictably, this fooled no one and, as he drifted towards the tragic end to his life, Lawrence was forced to take refuge behind his own myth. Thankfully, by then, this was so large a thing that he was able to stretch out behind it in reasonable comfort. Not a perfect end, perhaps, but better than nothing.

> **Lesson**: If you insist on becoming a legend, try to do so at night when fewer people will be able to see you.

[2] Trivia specialists and military anoraks will no doubt add that the enlisting officer was a pre-*Biggles* Capt. W.E. Johns.

# 47. KEITH!

Seafield Park, Keith, Banffshire

**NEED TO KNOW:** Mention the name Keith to the vast majority of people and they will reproduce for you in strident stereo the Alan Partridge radio commentary in which the said Keith pips to the post his equine rivals Thop Davity, Placenta Girl, Bishop Thumpity-Thump et al. A few doughty souls who dropped out of popular education classes to work down the mines might call to remembrance illustrious Keiths from the past such as Richards or Weller; while the defiantly esoteric might venture a Chegwin. Unhappily, they are all wrong, because the correct answer is Keith, Banffshire. For it is here that those in need of a summer retreat will find that the third beech up from the bench in the south-east corner of Seafield Park – home to the famous Keith Show (the whole park, that is, not just the bench) – will suit them just dandily.

**ADVANTAGES:** Once *in situ*, you command the whole of Keith. Not literally, of course – that would mean that the head of the local council would change every time someone climbed a tree overlooking the town. Calm yourself. It's merely an idiomatic expression suggesting that you enjoy a good view from up there, that's all.

**HAZARDS:** The lowest branch is about eight feet off the ground so you'll have to bring a ladder or an appropriately small crane. Moreover, should you fall asleep in the tree there is always the danger that autumn will arrive before you awake, leaving you in a beech denuded of all leaf life and surrounded by a group of mocking children pointing up at you and laughing (see **How to Hide in a Tree (ii)**, p. 160). Generally, the only thing to put a stop to this is to order them back to school. When this doesn't work, be violently ill on them.

## ESSENTIALS:

**LOCAL KNOWLEDGE:** Keith provides an excellent example of what Britain might have looked like had Drake not defeated the Spanish Armada and our Iberian friends had got busy imposing their town planning system throughout the nation. Its grid-iron street plan was laid out by the Earl of Findlater in 1750, presumably in an attempt to follow through this hypothesis.

**FREE FOOD:** Beech nuts. Stay in the tree long enough and you'll see them grow before your very eyes, leading you to believe in some deluded way that you know what it feels like to be a farmer.

**SUPPLIES:** The half-mile trek along Mid Street to The Deli Shop is worth it for the smell alone. Once you've had your olfactory fill (be reasonable and leave some for other customers), you might consider the dried leeks.

**PUBLIC CONVENIENCES:** In troubled Reidhaven Square, also called Keith Square, once called Market Place (all 0.25 miles).

**RECOMMENDED HIDURATION:**
2–3 days

**DIMENSIONS:**
4m x 3m

**COMFORT:**
3 Pleasant

**MAP REF:**
NJ 433 497

**OS LANDRANGER:** 28

COMPROMISED? Try *48. The Benches of Hard Knocks* (43 miles).

*All that is beyond the park is Keith. All that is Keith is yours. A self-portrait taken with your mobile is great art. Only one of these statements is true.*

# 48. THE BENCHES OF HARD KNOCKS

The Green, Aberdeen, Aberdeenshire

**NEED TO KNOW:** Aberdeen is a hard town. After all, it didn't earn the soubriquet 'The Granite City' on account of its fondness for debating the finer points of choreographic scores. This is the city that gave us the iron lung. It is a place of lantern-jawed men and Rosie the Riveter women. A city where they eat their young. Crawling under a pair of municipally owned seats such as *The Benches of Hard Knocks* is not unusual behaviour in Aberdeen. It is just the sort of thing that hard people do because they can. If you do likewise no one will take the slightest notice of you. If they register your existence at all, they will merely assume that you are Aberdonian yourself and leave you to it. It's one of the many benefits of living in a hard town.

That's what they'd like you to believe, anyway. The reality – like hell in that quote by Sartre, only in the singular – is somewhat other. It's the old old story: hard on the outside, mushy as a greetings card poem on the inside. The truth is, the people of Aberdeen are the gentlest beings in the whole of Scotland. Imagine a cross between a Care Bear, My Little Pony and a pink jelly baby and you're not even half-way there. Visualise instead those three all stuffed into a food mixer with lashings of condensed milk and blended to a sloppy pulp. Pour the resultant pap inside the softest human skin you can find and you've created your very own Aberdonian, albeit one of the tougher kinds. Therefore, if any of these tender creatures should become aware of your presence beneath the benches, far from ignoring you because it is accepted behaviour in the city, they will give you a wide berth, assuming you're an outsider from some tough town like Inverness or Tobermory. The result is, happily, the same – you are left in peace to hide for as long as you wish. Less happily, 'as long as you wish' may not turn out to be all that long because it's a wee bit uncomfortable down there.

**ADVANTAGES:** If it rains, folk will timorously hand you their umbrella before running away again.

**HAZARDS :** None of the above is true (except the first bit).

**ESSENTIALS :**

**LOCAL KNOWLEDGE:** They eat their young! They eat their young!

**FREE FOOD:** If you're lucky, the first things that come to the locals' hands as you run the gauntlet will be rotting fruit and veg. If you catch these right, you can usually burrow through them with your hands and find some sufficiently uncorrupted part to eat.

**SUPPLIES:** Most Aberdonians buy their victuals from ironmongers. You will find most of these indigestible except for perhaps the smallest parts of light fittings.

**PUBLIC CONVENIENCES:** Don't use any – you'll get mugged for your penny, for heaven's sake.

**MAKING A QUICK GETAWAY :**

**TRAIN:** Train! Train! Run for the train! The station's just a two-minute sprint away. Look not to the left or the right. Discard all jewellery. Give them anything they want. Just put your head down and go.

**COMPROMISED?** Go anywhere.

**RECOMMENDED HIDURATION:**
8–10 hours

**DIMENSIONS:**
2m x 0.8m
x 0.5m

**COMFORT:**
7 Plangent

**MAP REF:**
NJ 942 061

**OS LANDRANGER:** 38

*Add a pool of your own blood to the foreground and this is your likely first view if you ever regain consciousness.*

159

# HOW TO HIDE IN A TREE (II)

To the inexperienced hideur or hideuse, one tree might seem as good as the next when a few hours' seclusion is the dish chosen from life's rich banquet. However, as anyone who has fallen out of a holly tree will tell you, this is a grave error of judgement. Trees, like many people, are different and should be treated accordingly.

Expertise with regards to the troublesome question of *which tree when* can be gained in two ways. One can either commit the following straight-forward guidelines to memory and march with confidence into any coppice, spinney or arboretum in the land; or learn through suffering the embarrass-ment of having small children tug at their mother's skirt to enquire: 'Mater, what is that man doing sitting in that tree? Is he not aware that the austere yet artless figure he cuts has a certain *arriviste* vulgarity to it?' The choice is yours.

**Common yew** (*Taxus baccata*)
Often found in cemeteries, the doughty yew has been known to live for up to 2,000 years. It is there-fore ideal for those hiders who might be unnerved by being in a tree at the moment of its death. Tricky to climb due to its flattened spiky needles. Probably best to leave well alone and take cover behind a gravestone.

**Leyland cypress** (*x Cupressocyparis leylandii*)
Another evergreen, this tree is most often encoun-tered in the form of a hedge in suburban gardens, where its speed of growth is prized by those who would rather operate on their own spleen without anaesthetic than exchange a pleasantry with a neighbour. A hybrid of the true and false cypresses, of course, this is an excellent tree for just sort of wadging yourself into and standing there.

**English oak** (*Quercus robur*)
Particularly prevalent in the English Midlands, the oak has been specially designed with a large open-ing in its trunk that will admit one or more persons (see *14. Hollow Inside, Rather Like an Easter Egg*). Any oaks that do not have such an opening are defective and should be reported to the Forestry Commission without delay so that they can be separated from the herd and eaten by leopards.

**London plane** (*Platanus x hispanica*)
So called because it was first discovered growing on the runways at Croydon Airport, this tree is best approached with a ladder or tall wardrobe since it does not care to provide the would-be occupant with low-lying branches for easy access to its pleasingly concealing foliage above. It is said that 'He who hides in London Plane / Will not ever be seen again', but this may just be hearsay.

**Horse chestnut** (*Aesculus hippocastanum*)
A reliable old friend, the horse chestnut is the tree of choice for the professional hider with its candelabra flowers, enormous oval leaflets and rigorous interior logic. However, contrary to popular belief, one should never attempt to hide a horse in a horse chestnut. The small-leaved lime is much better suited to this purpose. In autumn, beware conkerers.

# 49. THE TURRET

nr The Hossack, Thurso East, Caithness

**NEED TO KNOW:** Almost anywhere in northern Scotland makes for a passable hiding place, for in comparison with the rest of Britain it is positively denuded of human life. Even in metropolitan Thurso (population c. 12,000), the High Street on a Sunday afternoon hustles and bustles with all the fervour of the *Marie Celeste*. Saunter to the eastern edge of town and even this amount of hustlage/bustlage becomes a rarity. It is therefore important not to impose your foreign ways on the place by acting as if you existed. Conversely, try to arrive as if you and your bodily presence were in fact somewhere completely different. Many experienced hiders prepare themselves psychologically for such an entrance by picturing themselves somewhere that is more properly described as nowhere much, such as Croydon. With their inner id inhabiting this shadowland, their bodies barely ripple their physical surroundings. It's really quite wonderful to behold, but don't try it at home in case you scare the cat.

**ADVANTAGES:** *The Turret* gives the appearance of having been erected by collecting some stones from the beach and casting them in concrete. As a consequence of this rather slapdash approach to construction, it is now in such a state of dereliction that there is no reason for anyone to want to come and see it. Likewise, the castle behind it has long since been breeze-blocked up and left to fall into the sea. Even the maps from the tourist information centre refer to the structure as 'Thurso Castle (site of)' which, given the fact that it's still quite clearly there, seems a bit harsh.

**HAZARDS:** It may be a tad exposed to the south-west, but this is nothing the donning of a concrete-coloured shell suit can't put right (for more super tips like this, see **The Art of Camouflage**, p. 56).

## ESSENTIALS:

**LOCAL KNOWLEDGE:** Thurso possesses Britain's most northerly train station, and every so often a train will get lost and end up here. Such visitations are gala occasions when the whole town turns out dressed in traditional costume of bunting and flagstones.

**FREE FOOD:** Short of eating the beach, there's not much to be done but starve. Sorry.

**SUPPLIES:** The closest purveyors of anything of substance are a hardware supplier and a coal merchant just up the River Thurso (0.2 miles). If this doesn't scratch you where you itch, there are scores of shopkeepers in the town (0.8 miles) with pointy sticks at the ready – a reassuring thought in troubled times.

**RECOMMENDED HIDURATION:**
3–5 hours

**DIMENSIONS:**
2m diameter

**COMFORT:**
3 Pleasant

**MAP REF:**
ND 125 691

**OS LANDRANGER:** 12

**PUBLIC CONVENIENCES:** Just by the same tourist information centre (0.7 miles) that wrote off Thurso Castle, so be ready for the toilets to be boarded up and hounded out of existence at a moment's notice.

**URBAN MYTH:** Local man and three times World Champion Hider, Houston O'Michaels, famously uses the so called 'Croydon Technique' to make himself appear as a ghost carrying his own head. For a fee he can do luminescence and a slightly foetid smell, which one witness has described as 'like that of a burning herring'.

## MAKING A QUICK GETAWAY:

**FERRY:** Wait until a train comes in and then sneak away through the festive crowd and get a boat out of town.

### COMPROMISED?

Since you're on the ferry already, you might as well try
*50. The Yesnaby Battery* (29 miles).

*Nothing between you and the North Pole but an exhausting and unlikely swim.*

# 50. THE YESNABY BATTERY

nr Yesnaby, Mainland, Orkney

**NEED TO KNOW:** 'War ... (Huh)?' as Edwin Starr so pertinently enquired, 'What is it good for?' Certainly not organic forms of architecture. This is why Gaudí was never asked to design a coastal gun emplacement. Or perhaps Franco did ask him and he turned him down. You'll have to look it up. Anyway, *Yesnaby Battery* is another fine example of the triumph of the functional over the aesthetic in the no-nonsense world of the military installation. Still, when hiding, 'functional' can mean the difference between a good night's sleep and double pneumonia (which apparently means you get it in both lungs, ordinary pneumonia merely being the bacterial inflammation of a single lung – I expect doctors thought it sounded better than telling people suffering from the latter that they only had half-pneumonia, especially if they went on to die from it), so set aside your exquisite taste in structural design for a moment and enjoy the whole four-walls-and-a-ceiling aspect of it that comprised almost the entirety of the architect's brief – that and it being able to with-stand a direct hit from a 6-inch shell.

**ADVANTAGES:** There are two further smaller buildings (not pictured) in case you fancy something a bit cosier or just feel downright guilty living in such a large place when so many people in the world are homeless. Furthermore, Orkney consists of no fewer than 70 islands, many of which are uninhabited and on which you could remain more or less indefinitely, at one at last with the dolphins, the seals and the porpoise who appears friendly but is really only humouring you.

**HAZARDS:** The ghost of Dirk McBattery, after whom the gun emplacement is named, has been known to appear out of the sea mist on winter mornings. A shepherd in life, McBattery is believed to have been killed in a freak mis-spelling disaster when a grenadine he was peeling went off in his hand. His appearance is said to bring mixed blessings for greengrocers, with a downturn in sales of exotic fruit but a rise in needless apostrophe's.

## ESSENTIALS:

**LOCAL KNOWLEDGE:** Just three miles up the coast is Skara Brae, which is a fantastic prehistoric village but rubbish for hiding in because none of the walls go much higher than three feet – this is probably the main reason why our prehistoric ancestors are no longer with us.

**FREE FOOD:** Rather than picking the rare Scottish primroses, develop a taste for sandstone. (Though having said that, better not, since it's falling into the sea as it is. Pick yourself up something nice from the Stromness Deli instead.)

**SUPPLIES:** The Stromness Deli (5 miles) specialises in food for those who would rather not add to the erosion of the coastline by wolfing down huge quantities of sandstone.

**RECOMMENDED HIDURATION:**
4–6 days

**DIMENSIONS:**
5.5m x 18m x 4m

**COMFORT:**
2 Plummy

**MAP REF:**
HY 221 162

**OS LANDRANGER:** 6

**PUBLIC CONVENIENCES:** A strange world, lost to itself, on the front at Stromness.

## MAKING A QUICK GETAWAY:

**FERRY:** There are any number of ferries that will whisk you off the island. Such is the enthusiasm of the ferry industry in Orkney that some of them go to places that haven't been discovered yet.

## COMPROMISED? Try 49. The Turret (29 miles).

*Similar to the view out to sea, only with fewer grenadines.*

# HIDING IN WALES

*Wales.*

Personally, I like the Welsh. Everyone says they have a chip on their shoulder and live in conditions of filth and despair (which is true) but they have a certain brittle quality to them that is wholly admirable. Some peoples (the Hungarians and Greeks spring to mind), when they break, seem merely to crumple up like a man unexpectedly slumping dead into a favourite armchair: the Welsh, however, shatter like chandeliers hurled into a furnace. It's as spectacular as it is tuneful, and a lot more fun. Furthermore, their homeland (better not call it a principality while you're enjoying their hospitality, it tends to rankle) is chock-full of prime hiding country awaiting the fortunate man or woman who takes their concealment seriously and doesn't mind the odd splinter of chandelier through the foot.

In a corracle, Wales comprises four different categories of land mass: Mountains, Coast, Abandoned mines and Other. The successful hider will learn to work in harmony with the particular foibles of each, since the only factor all four have in common is rain.

## Mountains

For a small country[1] Wales has a superabundance of mountains (roughly one per head of population), all of which make ripping places to hide since they are too cold and lonely for any life form but sheep. The mountains of Wales come in different varieties: Snowdonian ones in the north-west; Breconian ones in the south; Black ones either side of the Breconian ones; and Cambrian ones more or less everywhere else. Only the Welsh know the difference between these sorts of mountains, so you would be advised to ask a local what kind your chosen mountain is before going up into it. If it's a Black mountain, take a torch.

## Coast

Unlike some countries that faff around with fjords (Norway) or icebergs (Greenland), or others that have simply forgotten to order any coastline at all (Switzerland, Bolivia, Chad et al), Wales is content with good honest beaches and craggy rockiness. Where there are rocks, of course, a cave cannot be far away, and at the back of every good cave there is darkness. Darkness is the hider's friend. Come to the coast of Wales and enjoy the darkness.

## Abandoned mines

No one mines in Wales any more, least of all for coal. This is because, one Tuesday, all the miners moved away to work in Patagonia. This has left a lot of abandoned mines, most of which are completely dark. Darkness is the hider's friend etc., etc.

## Other

Everywhere in Wales that is not a mountain, coast or abandoned mine can be classified as other. Other is equivalent to an area twice the size of Wales. No, not really, that would be ridiculous. There's actually about two square foot of other in the middle of Anglesey. Don't bother trying to hide there, though: it's been fenced off by the MOD, and rightly so.

[1] For many years, Wales has been the undisputed king of nations favoured by journalists and documentary-makers who seek to bring the unimaginable into the realm of the imaginable – *viz.*: '16,000 square miles of Amazon rainforest – *that's about twice the size of Wales* – is lost every four seconds.' Unfortunately, this otherwise helpful scheme breaks down when trying to describe Wales itself, *bis viz.*: 'Wales is 8,016 square miles – *that's about the size of Wales* – and is lost every four seconds, though found again almost immediately.' If you wish to picture just how big Wales is, your only recourse is to imagine the area of Amazon rainforest that is lost every four seconds, then halve it.

# 51. NOT ANGELS BUT ANGLES

**Chapel Bay, Angle, Pembrokeshire/Sir Benfro**

**NEED to KNOW:** Unlike the *Yesnaby Battery* (see p. 164), *Not Angels* is built into a cliff-side rather than perched on top of one. It once protected Milford Haven from the incursions of those who would have sought to turn us all into muscular blond/e types for whom a dip in an icy lake before breakfast was just the fillip before a vigorous day's work on new theories of eugenics. Guns removed, buildings abandoned, the battery rests not so much on its laurels as underneath them, or would do, if someone had thought to plant some amid the sylvan counterpane that now shrouds the former dog of war.

**ADVANTAGES:** With its four spacious rooms, sentry box and gun emplacement, the erstwhile military installation makes an ideal hiding place for those who wish to hide en masse. Indeed, should you and the inhabitants of your compact but bifurcated village all need to hide at the same time, but not from each other, *Not Angels* could prove a lifesaver.

**HAZARDS:** The collapse of the Third Reich has meant that repairs here have not been a priority, so do not expect the flushing toilets, two-way tele-phony apparatus and open-ended badinage of its heyday. One of the rooms is also home to a colony of bats. These are amicable creatures, and should they spend the entire night dive-bombing you and defecating on your trousers, this should be taken as a sign of friendship. The entrance is a tad boggy too, even in summer.

**ESSENTIALS:**

**LOCAL KNOWLEDGE:** Best to avoid the first Saturday in August when the annual Angle Regatta brings an unwelcome influx of boats, fireworks and, if the posters are to be believed, sumo wrestlers to the area. On the off-chance that you have a quiz show to go to afterwards, keep in mind that Milford Haven is a glacial ria.

**FREE FOOD:** The seaweed on the shore below may be converted into laver bread (see **Plant Life and How to Eat It**, p. 106) but may remain just where it is.

**SUPPLIES:** The Village Store in Angle (0.5 miles) purveys sweets in jars.

**PUBLIC CONVENIENCES:** Opposite St Mary's Church, Angle.

**RECOMMENDED HIDURATION:**
Up to 7 days

**DIMENSIONS:**
50m x 12m

**COMFORT:**
1 Plush

**MAP REF:**
SM 863 036

**OS LANDRANGER:** 157

## MAKING A QUICK GETAWAY:

**BUS:** The 387 is a 'hail and ride' bus which will take you in a circle from Angle (0.5 miles) to Pembroke, Lamphey (famous for its doughnuts) and back. Two in each direction daily. Meanwhile, the 366 runs twice to Pembroke Dock, though only once via Waterloo.

**TRAIN:** Pembroke (8.5 miles) for Tenby. Milford Haven (3 miles across the water, somewhat further by land) for Fishguard and the sea. Either for Swansea and Mid-Wales.

**SHIP:** If your story is a sorry enough one, doubtless some kind captain will take you aboard his ship without necessarily selling you into slavery at the next port. A more conventional service sails twice daily from Pembroke to Rosslare (3 hours 45 minutes).

## COMPROMISED?  Try *52. Slot* (14 miles).

*An oil tanker – its existence your doing, its depredations the fruit of your licentiousness.*

# 52. SLOT

Priest's Nose, Manorbier, Pembrokeshire/Sir Benfro

**NEED to KNOW:** Differing rates of erosion have formed a slot in the cliffs wide enough to lie down in, entirely secreting the occupier from view. The hider is then afforded the opportunity of enjoying no fewer than three strata of Old Red Sandstone – Shrinkle Sandstone, Ridgeway Conglomerate and Red Marls – each fascinating in their own way for up to three minutes. Roughly half a mile from the nearest habitation, *Slot* is ideal for the casual hider with no previous history of arthritis.

**ADVANTAGES:** If rumbled, there are escape routes inland, east and west along the coastal path and, *in extremis*, seaward.

**HAZARDS:** Stray walkers descending from the coastal footpath. Weather can be a trifle fierce in winter. Prone to waterlogging at all times of year.

**ESSENTIALS:**

**LOCAL KNOWLEDGE:** The water quality off this stretch of coast is such that it has earned the prized Blue Flag. However, it should be noted that although this means the water is very clean, it may still prove a little salty for most tastes. Surfers all year round (not Christmas Day or Third in Trinity).

**FREE FOOD:** Coltsfoot – a vital ingredient in those hard sticks that used to be de rigueur in sweet shops, but less appetising eaten by itself. Nice cheery colour though. Furthermore, the plentiful rock samphire hereabouts can be made into a pickle at a moment's notice. Those requiring a full ploughman's, however, should remember to bring their own cheese, bread, butter and pickled onion.

**SUPPLIES:** A mini-super/post office on the main road through Manorbier (0.8 miles) is staffed by some of the friendliest people in Manorbier.

**PUBLIC CONVENIENCES:** At Manorbier Bay car park (0.4 miles).

**RECOMMENDED HIDURATION:**
2–4 hours

**DIMENSIONS:**
8m x 0.7m

**COMFORT:**
8 Plaguey

**MAP REF:**
SS 061 970

**OS LANDRANGER:** 158

## MAKING A QUICK GETAWAY:

**BUS:** Eleven buses a day will whisk you either to Haverfordwest or Tenby (reduced service Sundays).

**TRAIN:** Copious trains from Manorbier station (1.75 miles) to Pembroke Dock, from where an ocean-going liner may be purchased or stowed away upon, according to budget.

**COMPROMISED?** Try the hole in the cliffs a few hundred yards to the east (SS 065 970).

*The sea. Imagine the old man and the sea. Now take away the old man.*

# WHAT TO DO WHILE HIDDEN

For many hiders, whether they seclude themselves out of necessity or merely for pleasure, the most pressing problem is not the hiding per se, but what to do while hidden. A minute can often seem like an hour; an hour, a day. Which of us, after an afternoon's good concealment, has not looked at his or her watch to discover that a measly five minutes has passed? As the children's skipping rhyme has it: 'In the hollow of a tree or the far corner of a disused air-raid shelter, time can hang very heavy indeed.'

If you are hiding in tandem or in a group, such a difficulty is easily resolved. Assuming there is no danger of anyone from the non-hidden world overhearing, you may simply indulge yourselves in pleasant conversation, perhaps over a glass or two of warmed milk and brandy. Worthwhile and

*No, no, no.*

enriching topics might include: i) What I did in my half-term holidays; ii) The consolation of footwear; iii) Getting to grips with gravel; or iv) How does a sheep? Subjects to be avoided include anything of a purely philosophical nature. For example, any exchange centring on the question 'If we were both starving to death would you give me your last biscuit?' is likely to end in recriminations. It should go without saying, but in these confused times it will not do any harm to emphasise it here, that on no account should the conversation veer towards the actual act of hiding embarked on at that moment, since this is still seen in most circles as rather gauche and the sort of practice in which beginners, wastrels and the generally unsound are wont to indulge. Do not show your-self up.

For lone hiders – those practising what most would agree to be the purest form of the art – the problem is less easily wrestled into submission. A conversation with oneself might at first manifest itself as a fulfilling and frequently enlightening experience but, more often than not, it is a path that leads all too rapidly to despair, madness and, finally, some act of unspeakable degradation. Remember, it is rarely a happy thing to make yourself a taboo subject within your own family.

What, then, is left for the man or woman hiding *in tod sloaniam*, as our Roman cousins had it? Not much, is the sad answer. Given that most ordinary hobbies or pastimes are impractical in the often confined and under-resourced settings of a hidey-hole – for example, very few successful hiders have passed the hours giving free expression to their fondness for paragliding – the subject must fall back on simpler, unadorned pleasures. A pack of cards can give hours of enjoyment, especially if opened. Reading, too, can be a satisfying means of whiling away the odd hour while incommunicado. However, care should be taken in the selection of the book. Anything too large and there is a possibility of it becoming irretrievably wedged in one of the smaller entrances to the nation's places of hidingness, and this will do nobody any good, least of all you. Conversely, anything too small and it may not be able to hold enough words. There are few things more frustrating than getting half way through a novel only to reach the last page.

Of course, many people see hiding as an end in itself and consider such amusements as distractions from the task at hand. Still others look upon a period of concealment as a time in which they can cut themselves off from all diversions in order to engage in some healthy introspection (see also **What to Think**, p. 194). This is a laudable approach to take as long as such soul-searching extends up to but does not include the point where you begin to have conversations with yourself in which you refer to yourself as 'we' (*viz.*, 'Aren't we the lucky one?'), only to refer to yourself in the third person singular in reply (*viz.*, 'Of course, he would know, wouldn't he, because he's always right.').

In summary: to hide is to do. Is that not enough?

# SCENES FROM THE WORLD OF SECLUSION

## nr *1. All Mine*

*A rare confluence of hiding places – a waterside cavelet lurks beneath an abandoned engine house. Astonishingly, neither is aware that the other is there.*

# 53. THE SHIELD

nr Oxwich, The Gower, Glamorgan/Morgannwg

**NEED to KNOW:** A magnificent rocky outcrop – positioned where a particularly creative child might imagine a big toe to be if the Gower Peninsula were a gargantuan foot – appears, from a distance, to provide most infertile soil for the hider. However, the child has also imagined some sort of rare fungal growth on the nail of the big toe which affords a measure of secrecy and shelter even as it gives the child's parents the first inkling that all may not be right with the light of their lives.

**ADVANTAGES :** The grassy ledge is protected by a cliff face behind and several wind-sculpted blackthorn bushes in front. The bewitching view offers ample warning of pursuers, whether on land or in the Bristol Channel. The former would also find themselves severely inconvenienced by the deceptively brutal screen of gorse covering the southern approaches. The latter, for some reason, are in boats on the Bristol Channel and so pose little threat.

**HAZARDS :** The brutal screen of gorse may at first seem somewhat daunting, while just a few seconds in its barbed and bristly grasp are enough to educate the trespasser as to the extent of its deceptiveness. However, persevere and you will at length perceive a sort of rabbit track passing through the gorse which makes its transit a little less like being attacked by a mob of syringe-happy octo-puses.

**LOCAL KNOWLEDGE:** Towards the end of World War II, the wrecking of an oil tanker denuded the area of cockles so, unless you plan to hide here before 1945, any attempt to study them *in situ* is likely to prove unrewarding.

**SUPPLIES:** A clutch of Oxwichian stores (1 mile) will happily equip you with food, buckets and a selection of Welsh handicrafts. If you are contemplating a lengthy stay there is no need to shop for wool, since stray sheep are wont to leave scraps of their outer garment on the blackthorn. A makeshift loom can be readily constructed using spare branches, braided hair and amalgam fillings melted down and fashioned into nails. If prisoners in Colditz could build such devices under the noses of the German Wehrmacht, it shouldn't be beyond you.

**PUBLIC CONVENIENCES:** Opposite the Oxwich Bay Hotel (0.8 miles).

**RECOMMENDED HIDURATION:**
2–3 days

**DIMENSIONS:**
2m x 5m

**COMFORT:**
4 Placid

**MAP REF:**
SS 507 849

**OS LANDRANGER** 159

## MAKING A QUICK GETAWAY :

**BUS:** From Oxwich Cross (1 mile), nine buses a day connect with services to Swansea. Other rhyming destinations such as Rhossili and Killey are also catered for, though more sporadically.

**BOAT:** Something small and sprightly could easily put in at The Sands, a tiny cove 1.5 miles west, and leave with you on board.

## COMPROMISED?

Try *56. The Amphitheatre* (23 miles).

*The Oxwich Promontory – note rare fungal growth (centre left).*

177

# 54. THE WETNESS OF THINGS

Bute Park/Coopers Field, Cardiff/Caerdydd, Glamorgan/Morgannwg

**NEED TO KNOW:** There seems to be some dispute as to whether the greenery just here is called Bute Park or Coopers Field. There's a good chance that one is a subset of the other, so it may be that both warring parties are right and that the bloodshed and general carnage of the last 500 years has been largely needless. It's probably best to declare yourself a neutral when visiting, although this may make you a figure of suspicion to both sides. All the more reason for making yourself scarce, a feat that can be carried out with some aplomb here under this bridge over the (usually) dry bed of a man-made tributary that (occasionally) feeds the Afon Taf. 'Why build an occasional man-made tributary into the Taf?', I hear you cry, and it is a question not without merit. The answer is that it's more of an attempted moat than anything else, for aye, yet again we find that a castle has grown up around a conspicuously (by which, in the hiding world, we mean inconspicuously) fine place to conceal oneself.

**ADVANTAGES:** The space under the bridge is heroically peaceful yet only a minute's walk from the Millennium Stadium (so called because it is one of a thousand similar stadia built around the country), wherein you may dance to the sounds of popular recording artistes or marvel at one of the many sporting spectacles performed here by men and women trained especially for the purpose.

**HAZARDS:** Standing in about 18 inches of water is, admittedly, not everyone's idea of pleasure, no matter that the water does look reasonably clean at first. Also, in the rainy season (which began in Wales in 1355), there is a possibility that this water could rise, causing the skin of long-term hiders to go all tabby (by which, sadly, we mean 'wrinkly' rather than 'like a cat' which would be fantastic and would improve your social standing no end, especially with cats).

## ESSENTIALS:

**LOCAL KNOWLEDGE:** 'King' Caractacus – renowned for a Court that was for ever 'just passing by' – was a local leader of the Silures who was forcibly exiled by the Romans. His rightful place in history was restored in the 20th century by Rolf Harris, the celebrated campaigner on Silurian issues.

**FREE FOOD:** Springtime daffodils offer a mouthful of sustenance. This can be supplemented by the mouthful you'll get from the park-keeper if he catches you eating them.

**SUPPLIES:** The Wales Centre in Castle Street (0.1 miles) contains all manner of food to which the prefix 'Welsh' has been added, presumably as a warning.

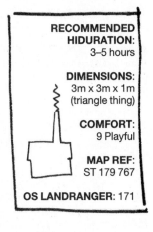

**RECOMMENDED HIDURATION:**
3–5 hours

**DIMENSIONS:**
3m x 3m x 1m
(triangle thing)

**COMFORT:**
9 Playful

**MAP REF:**
ST 179 767

**OS LANDRANGER:** 171

**PUBLIC CONVENIENCES:** Just around the corner in Kingsway (0.2 miles). Alternatively, buy an annual ticket to Cardiff Castle (0.1 miles) and use theirs.

**COMPROMISED?** Try *53. The Shield* (72 miles).

*The moat – like the levee to which Don McLean drove his Chevy – is dry.*

# GUNTHER PLÜSCHOW
## (1886–1931)

> **Hiduration**: 9 days
>
> **Value as role model**: 10/10

The fact that Gunther Plüschow is better known in this country as 'Gunther Who?' is testament to the aphorism that the history books are written by the victors. Had Plüschow found himself flying in the RFC rather than its German equivalent, no doubt his exploits would long since have been made into a Hollywood musical without which Christmas Day is simply not Christmas Day. As it is, he has had to content himself with being the only German prisoner of war ever to make a home run from a British camp. In doing so, he ran the whole gamut of the hiding arts from disguise to deception to plain unadulterated getting-out-of-everyone's-way. By the time all this came about – July 1915 – he had already become the first (and only as it turned out) German to escape from Kiao-Chow, a German protectorate in China besieged by our then friends the Japanese. He was eventually captured by the British at Gibraltar as he tried to make it back to Germany on a steamer from New York posing as a wealthy British businessman. Interned at Donington Hall Camp in the Midlands, Plüschow's thoughts soon turned to the business of evading the dastardly Brits.

His escape plan was fairly rudimentary. He and one Oberleutnant Trefftz crept into a sort of grotto affair in the grounds of Donington Hall and hid beneath some garden chairs. When night came they emerged from the grotto, scaled the three fences, changed into civilian mackintoshes and wandered off down the road. The only hiccup came when Plüschow lost the seat of his trousers on some barbed wire and had to retrieve the patch of dislodged material in order to sew it back in later.

Guided by the Pole star (and the occasional road sign), they reached Derby at four in the morning and, no doubt, began to wish they'd never left the camp. Undeterred, however, they sneaked into someone's garden and had a shave in the (well founded) conviction that the English believed that only dirty foreigners and the undeserving poor went about unshaven and so to do so would arouse suspicion.

The two parted company at Derby station. Plüschow cannily bought a single to Leicester, where he got off the train and purchased a London ticket. Thus, when enquiries were made by the camp authorities at Derby about unusual characters buying single tickets to London, the ticket clerk didn't call him to mind.

For his first night in London, Plüschow found a hiding place in what he described as an 'aristocratic lane' which must have been somewhere near Hyde Park. He hopped over a fence and fell asleep under a thick box hedge. He awoke to find a policeman wandering up and down the pavement just inches from his nose but kept his cool and waited for the upstanding officer of the law to be distracted by a charming young slip of a lady's maid before making a hasty exit.

He quickly formed the opinion that during the hours of darkness it would be less hazardous to pass himself off as 'a tramp', and so spent the second night sleeping in Hyde Park with a group of homeless gentlemen. The next day, he learnt from the headlines at a newspaper stand that his friend Trefftz had been recaptured and that the police were hot on his own trail. He promptly bought a newspaper and read a description of his 'smart and dapper' appearance. Naturally, he immediately changed said appearance as much as possible, although there was little he could do about his 'very good teeth', something the police were very keen to have publicised. Indeed, the boys in blue were on to something there, for if his teeth were even half-decent they would have been the best set of gnashers in Britain at the time, so one can only imagine that Plüschow spent the following seven days desperately anxious not to smile inadvertently and so give himself away.

In the meantime, he had become 'a docker on strike' – discarding any clothes mentioned in the newspaper report, colouring his blond hair black with Vaseline, bootblack and coal dust, and spreading yet more coal on his clothes. Apparently, striking dockers (didn't they know there was a war on?) frequently covered themselves in coal to further their cause, a practice now considered passé by today's disenchanted workers.

On the top deck of a bus, Plüschow providentially overheard a conversation during which he learnt that a Dutch steamer departed from Tilbury for Flushing in Holland at seven each morning. He rushed off to Tilbury and, posing as a sailor (a grubby one, presumably), he staked out the good ship *Mecklenburg* (by a happy coincidence, also the name of his birthplace).

It was time to create a hiding place from where he could make his dash to board the ship. He crossed the river to Gravesend and found some planks under a bridge, beneath which he fortuitously came across some bundles of comfy warm hay. In hiding terms, this is about as good as it gets. Sadly, the hay has since been removed.

From here he made three attempts on three separate nights to get on board the *Mecklenburg*. The first one nearly killed him – the tide was out, so he waded towards the ship but almost sank without trace in the mud before he'd gone ten yards. His second stab at it involved the theft of an old rowing boat which almost immediately sank beneath him. The third attempt, however, like in all the best fables, was a success. Plüschow half-inched (he was getting the hang of Cockney rhyming slang by now) a dinghy and drifted downstream to a bridge. Here he lay in the long grass all the next day until it was dark. He then drifted back upstream on the incoming tide, before rowing out to the buoy to which the *Mecklenburg* was attached. It was then just a matter of hauling himself up the steel cable to the hawse and tumbling into the forecastle. In those days, fortunately, hauling oneself up an almost vertical steel cable in the dark above a swiftly flowing river was not considered particularly hazardous or indeed difficult.

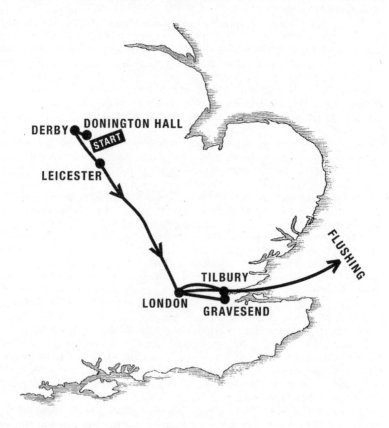

Our hero hid himself in one of the ship's lifeboats and, in true *Boy's Own* style, feeling no fear fell fast asleep. He awoke in Flushing, where he calmly slipped his boots on and sauntered down the gangway, this time posing as a member of the crew. At the dock, however, he was faced with another potential hazard – the customs office.

The Dutch may be jolly good at football and first-rate clog-makers and all that, but in 1915 their customs officials were not the brightest bunnies in the warren. On a door near their checkpoint they had placed a sign reading 'Exit Forbidden'. Naturally enough, the *Mecklenburg*'s newest crew member sallied through it and evaded the lot of them.

Plüschow bought some clothes and the next day boarded a train for Germany dressed as a workman. Before long he was over the border and heading into the record books, if not into the annals of British history.

---

**Lesson**: If at first you don't succeed, try, try again.

No, hang on, that was someone else.

---

# 55. STONES

**the left bank of the Afon Teifi, nr Castle Emlyn, Newcastle Emlyn,
Carmarthenshire/Sir Gaerfyrddin**

**NEED to KNOW:** The 'Rive Gauche' of the Teifi has long since established itself
as the trendy side of the river with its rich tapestry of foot-
paths, bench-life and grass. However, do not let its current vogueishness sway you
into dismissing it out of hand as a possible venue at which to disappear for a while.
Not only is this particular location rather tricky to get at (see 'Advantages'), the cover
afforded by the beech and laurel above make it ideal for lovers of fine cuisine (see
'Free food').

**ADVANTAGES:** *Stones* (so called because, unlike other places such as sandy
beaches or pizza restaurants, it has some) is to be found on a
whiskerly thin island in the Teifi formed by the same erosive action that causes oxbow
lakes. Indeed, technically, the painfully modest slither of river you must cross by one
or other of the hilariously precarious bridges in order to gain the island is an oxbow
lake in the making.

**HAZARDS:** Some people – especially geography teachers – are apt to become
over-excited by features such as oxbow lakes, roches moutonnées
and bergschrunds (see **Where Not to Hide**, p. 188). If you suspect that yours is the
sort of personality type that is susceptible to splintering, cracking or forming into
scree in the event of a surprise encounter with lateral moraine or a U-shaped valley,
this may not be the place for you.

**LOCAL KNOWLEDGE:** Newcastle Emlyn was once home to Theophilus Evans (1693–1767), vicar of Llangamarch and penner of the first Welsh-language bestseller *Drych y Prif Oesoedd* (published in English as *A View of the Primitive Ages*). Some people – especially Welsh history teachers – are apt to become over-excited by this seminal account of the nation's formative years. If you suspect that yours is the sort of personality type that is susceptible to splintering, cracking or forming into endless rows of secondary clauses in the event of a surprise encounter with a massacre of 1,200 non-Papist monks, this may not be the place for you.

**RECOMMENDED HIDURATION:**
3–4 hours

**DIMENSIONS:**
2m x 3m

**COMFORT:**
6 Plebeian

**MAP REF:**
SN 312 408

**OS LANDRANGER:** 145

**FREE FOOD:** Toasted beech nuts, served on a laurel-leaf platter, make an appetising starter. This can be followed by a main course of beech *brûlé* with a laurel garnish and finished off – if the diet will allow – with a generous serving of *noix de beech au laurel*.

**SUPPLIES:** Hughes Gauge, the delicatessen on Sycamore Street (0.4 miles), will fulfil all of your puy-lentil demands, and possibly others besides.

**PUBLIC CONVENIENCES:** In the Market Building, a craggy island at the southern end of Sycamore Street (0.3 miles).

**COMPROMISED?** Try *56. The Amphitheatre* (15 miles).

*The famous Newcastle Emlyn Tree of Diplomacy stands neither on the left bank nor on the right bank. Indeed, getting any sort of opinion out of it is like trying to herd cats.*

# 56. THE AMPHITHEATRE

Priory Street, Carmarthen, Carmarthenshire/Sir Gaerfyrddin

**NEED TO KNOW:** A welcoming armchair is the sole piece of furniture in a room created by a privet tree. A carpet of ivy gives way to holly – the ascetic's friend – for a footstool. All this and a Roman amphitheatre at your beck, if not your call.

**ADVANTAGES:** Excellent all-weather coverage in a cosy armchair which may not contain as many fleas as it appears. Located right where the green room might well have been in the days when the amphitheatre rang to the uplifting soliloquies of Terence and Plautus. Two exits.

**HAZARDS:** The amphitheatre now doubles as a public park and so the occasional interloper should be expected. To combat this, try playing a recording of the distress call of the male howler monkey. This should leave you undisturbed for as long as you wish.

**ESSENTIALS:**

LOCAL KNOWLEDGE: Carmarthen (Moridunum) plays host to just over 14 per cent of all the Roman amphitheatres in Britain. This one would have seated an audience of 5,000 who would have whistled, jeered and heckled their way through various plays, mimes (short parodies in which, to everyone's relief, the actors were allowed to speak), pantomimes (performed by a single dancer, which doesn't sound much fun, though this may still be preferable to watching a minor TV celebrity bellowing 'Oh no he isn't' every three minutes for an hour and a half) and spectacles (there was nothing the Romanised Celts enjoyed more of an evening than watching a good pair of glasses). Football is the theatre of the 21st century, of course, and Carmarthen Town reached the second qualifying round of the UEFA Cup in 2005, going out to FC Copenhagen.

**FREE FOOD**: Rosehips.

**SUPPLIES**: Priory Potatoes, a greengrocer/off-licence opposite the entrance to the amphitheatre.

**PUBLIC CONVENIENCES**: In the car park on St Peter's Street, opposite the church (0.25 miles).

**PLAY TO PRODUCE**: *Happy Days* by Samuel Beckett. You are Winnie, up to her waist and, later, neck in mud but ever the optimist. In this production the futility of her/your existence is cleverly

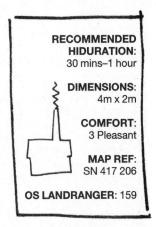

**RECOMMENDED HIDURATION:**
30 mins–1 hour

**DIMENSIONS:**
4m x 2m

**COMFORT:**
3 Pleasant

**MAP REF:**
SN 417 206

**OS LANDRANGER:** 159

emphasised by the dearth of publicity surrounding the event, thus ensuring that no one is there to witness it. After all, you are meant to be hiding, not changing the face of British theatre as we know it.

## MAKING A QUICK GETAWAY:

**BUS:** The stop is directly outside the amphitheatre and is patronised by buses hurtling towards Aberystwyth, Cardigan, Llandovery and Newcastle Emlyn, though not all at once.

**TRAIN:** Frequent service both north-west and south-east.

## COMPROMISED?

Try *55. Stones* (15 miles).

*First Soldier: Ecce! Ecce!*
*[Second Soldier does not look and is crushed to death by a homily.]*

# WHERE NOT TO HIDE

Knowing where to hide is a skill that takes a lifetime to master[1] and the whole business may, at first sight, seem rather a daunting prospect. However, it is possible to avoid some of the tears, traumas and temper tantra of the early years by learning first where *not* to hide.

Keeping a list in your head of locations that are an absolute no-no, you should be able to go through that first tricky decade with your toys more or less still inside the pram, or at least within an acceptable radius of it (see Fig. i).

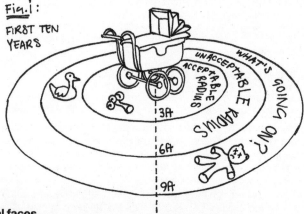

Fig. i:
FIRST TEN YEARS

## Vertical faces

Cliffs, the sides of buildings, sheer drops off mountain peaks – none of these are any good, for there's no arguing with gravity. Indeed, even come 2010, when each of us receives a government-issue personal anti-gravity pack, there will still be little point in choosing a vertical face as a place of concealment unless it's one that only you can get behind.

Size is not an issue here either. For instance, Orkney's St John's Head – Britain's tallest sea cliff – has a surface area of between three and four million square feet, and yet remains completely hopeless as a place to hide since every square inch is open to scrutiny by any Tom, Dick or Harriet (see horrible demise, below) who cares to take a boat out of Stromness. In fact it's a puzzle as to why the thing was ever built in the first place. One can only imagine it was some sort of Orcadian job creation scheme that went horribly awry. Avoid.

---

[1] So if you're middle-aged and just starting to learn, you're likely to become only mediocre to fair by the time you die. It's a dispiriting thought.

*Completely hopeless.*

## Horizontal faces

These are often harder to identify than vertical faces since they tend to make less of a song and dance about their presence, but are just as dangerous.

Typical British examples include: plains, fens, empty car parks and giant outdoor chessboards from which the pieces have been removed for the winter. Should you find yourself in foreign climes, steppe, tundra and veldt are all to be steered clear of. Veldt is particularly to be shunned. It's not for nothing that the old South African national anthem begins: 'I see the foreigner lying on the veldt / He thinks he is invisible / But I shoot him.'

## Places where things are deliberately mashed

This should be obvious, but there can hardly be an undertaker in the land who has not had to fill a coffin with bricks in order to disguise how little there was left of Tom, Dick or Harriet once the site foreman had managed to locate the emergency cut-out on the scrap-metal crusher. Other similar places to be avoided include dustcarts, waste-disposal units, industrial coffee-grinders and any machine bearing the word 'pulper' on the side.

In the natural world, a similarly wide berth should be given to berg-schrunds: the crevasses at the heads of glaciers or névés. These have an alarming habit of waiting for scientists with measuring gear to lower them-selves down them before snapping shut, flattening their hapless victims like slices of cucumber between two pieces of bread so hard and stale that you wouldn't even throw them out for the birds. If a bergschrund can do this to a scientist in a white coat and half-moon glasses, it is rash to imagine that it would have any more respect for you, especially in those dungarees.

# 57. HOLLY BOARD

Castell Warden, Warden Road, Llanandras/Presteigne, Radnorshire/Sir Faesyfed

**NEED TO KNOW:** At the foot of an 11th-century bailey, a lone holly tree grows. 'Neath the holly tree, a section of plywood, from the rare but useful plywood tree, is held upright by a strip of wood. The resulting coffin-sized shape resembles the space you might end up with if you, or someone like you, had been blessed with the ability to dig a slit trench above ground.

**ADVANTAGES:** The holly tree is rightly famed for its propensity to form an under-storey in beech woods. This is what is known in hiding parlance as 'double-glazing' – a state in which the hider is protected not just by one layer of protection but two (see also *40. Welcome to Glasgow*). The only danger in this is complacency. Those who seek shelter under holly trees that grow beneath a canopy of beech are apt to forget that neither species of tree has been shown to withstand a thorough dosing of napalm or Agent Orange, so before hiding in such places do make sure first that you know with what degree of sophistication your pursuers are likely to seek you out. Here, of course, there is nothing at all above the holly so complacency simply doesn't enter into it, unless you're the sort of person who is complacent about everything, in which case you are a danger to yourself and others and fully deserve to be found so that society can keep an eye on you. Unlike at most other hiding places, Christmas hiders need not bring their own holly.

**HAZARDS:** The *Holly Board* is situated next to what the Castell Warden notice board terms, a little breathlessly, a 'Danger Area'. However, the board is silent as to the precise nature of the danger so it may be propitious to guard against all possibilities. Most experienced hiders carry a penknife, inflatable dinghy and shoulder-held rocket-launcher at all times and you may be advised to follow suit.

**LOCAL KNOWLEDGE:** The castle 'was used by the Mortimers to tighten their grip on the Lugg Valley', though this is rarely a cause for concern except at busy times such as the May Bank Holidays and Assizes Day, on which selected members of the rival de Say family are taken to the former Shire Hall and publicly hanged.

**SUPPLIES:** In town (0.2 miles) there is a copious spread of miniature shops selling (more or less life-sized) food and drink. The building and agricultural supplies merchant is a good source of replacement strips of wood in the event that yours run out for some reason.

**PUBLIC CONVENIENCES:** Back Lane (0.4 miles). Left, over, onwards, right, fifth left.

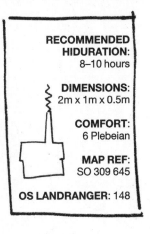

**RECOMMENDED HIDURATION:**
8–10 hours

**DIMENSIONS:**
2m x 1m x 0.5m

**COMFORT:**
6 Plebeian

**MAP REF:**
SO 309 645

**OS LANDRANGER:** 148

**MAKING A QUICK GETAWAY :**

**BUS:** Several buses ram the frontier between the Welsh and English nations. Ludlow may be gained once a day, Leominster and Shobdon four times as often. For those unwilling to risk the perils of the frontier, there's the tricky choice between Maesyfed and Tref-y-Clawdd.

**COMPROMISED?** Try *14. Hollow Inside, Rather Like an Easter Egg* (10 miles).

*This wood, skilfully hidden by radical conservationists, cannot be seen for the trees.*

# 58. OWAIN'S NOOK

**Aberystwyth Castle, Aberystwyth, Cardiganshire/Ceredigion**

**NEED to KNOW:** Some folk, their long wayward hair flowing in the first warm breeze of spring, view Aberystwyth as less of a name and more of a nomenclatury stammer. These are the very same people, however, who are wont to mispronounce 'otiose' and refer to the European Union as the Common Market, and so are best disregarded. Owain Glyndŵr, his wayward, largely uncon-ditioned, hair flowing in the first warm breeze of spring like an unruly flag of indepen-dence, held the castle only from 1404 to 1408 but no doubt hid in this very spot, if only to escape the attentions of troubadours who were always pestering him for stories of battle they could turn into 108-verse tone poems for lute and harpsichord.

**ADVANTAGES:** Aberystwyth's fine, if not wholly extant, castle is free for all to roam in. This, at first, may seem contrary to the hider's best interests. However, the good news is that what's left of Edward I's stronghold is on such an exposed salient of coastline that fewer people than you might expect actually exercise their right to scamper around on it, preferring instead the cosy warmth of the town's numerous tea shops or the self-generated warmth offered by some hurly-burly on the cliff-top frisbee golf course.

**HAZARDS:** You are still unsure if you yourself mispronounce otiose, in which case the chances are you do. Disregard yourself for a bit; it will probably be good for your soul in the long run.

**ESSENTIALS:**

**LOCAL KNOWLEDGE:** The first recorded use of cannon (fans of passing references to outmoded artillery pieces should also see p. 115, where they've a real treat awaiting them) on these isles occurred right here. By 'recorded', of course, we mean written down. Nobody thought it worth recording the sound of the cannon (cf. other irregular plurals: sheep, fish, series) until the emergence in the 1940s of bebop jazz, whose more avant garde practitioners incorporated them in lieu of bassoons. Anyway, the cheery old Prince of Wales, on his way to becoming Henry V and landing himself the title role in a brace of Shakespearean plays, waved away the doubters, the nay-sayers and the Luddites in his entourage and happily blasted away with the new-fangled cannon at the Welsh. Whose Prince he was. Tough love. Still, it didn't go completely belly-up for the castle until the Civil War when the Roundheads slighted it (a popular pastime in those days – see also *23. The Quatrefoil Tower*).

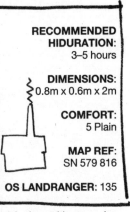

**RECOMMENDED HIDURATION:**
3–5 hours

**DIMENSIONS:**
0.8m x 0.6m x 2m

**COMFORT:**
5 Plain

**MAP REF:**
SN 579 816

**OS LANDRANGER:** 135

**FREE FOOD:** Hail and sleet, cooked properly, make a surprisingly nutritious meal.

**SUPPLIES:** Organic types should head for Treehouse, the organic shop/café/bar/restaurant in the chemical-free heart of town (0.3 miles).

**PUBLIC CONVENIENCES:** Right there in the castle grounds.

**URBAN MYTH:** Owain Glyndŵr kept his wife safe from the English by hiding her in his beard.

COMPROMISED? Try *59. The Trough* (43 miles).

*All castles in Britain were eventually replaced by the electric typewriter.*

# WHAT TO THINK

If there were such a thing as an existential alarm clock that awakened the sleeper by playing the Gauloise-treated voice of Jean-Paul Sartre reading snippets from *La Nausée*, his 1938 'oh dear, I'm not feeling at all well this week' *roman provocateur*, the law of averages would decree that one happy morning the slumberer would be stirred to consciousness by the following: 'My thought is *me*: that's why I can't stop. I exist by what I think ... and I can't prevent myself from thinking.'

The good news is that, despite the non-existence of such a clock (although rumours continue to circulate regarding a Romanian time-piece that uses a recording of his guest appearance as narrator on *The Magic Roundabout*), you can still let JPS be your wake-up call, and his call is this: 'I am what I think and if I stop thinking I cease to exist but I will not because I cannot prevent myself from thinking so I just carry on forever, or at least until such time as I die from an oedema of the lung and not, as is often thought, in a car crash: that was Camus.'

In a nutshell: self-analysis/angst/death.

**Self-analysis**
The hider is, by definition, a lone soul, a resolute individualist, a soliloquising widowed swan who, coming upon two roads that diverge in a wood, eschews the one less travelled by, preferring instead to throw himself in a ditch and wait for nightfall.

It is no surprise therefore to find that, when finally installed in blissful solitude, the thoughts of the vast majority of hiders naturally turn to self. Indeed, where better than beneath the waves of a lily pond, for instance, to ask '*Who am I? What am I doing?*' and '*How did I get here?*'

However, although a certain amount of introspection is healthy – the unexamined life not being worth living and all that – it is possible to go too far. You will know that this point has been reached when you begin to refer to yourself in the third person but to everything else as 'I' (for variations, see **What to Do While Hidden**, p. 172). From here it is a short journey into *Angst*.

**Angst**
Inevitably, even if the rate at which one peppers one's speech with unnecessary and often wholly inaccurate French may increase with a pleasing swiftness, the anxieties and cares of everyday life are far from being sloughed off when one enters *la vie clandestine*. The predominant concern for the hider, however, will always be the likelihood of discovery by a third party. This can lead to all sorts of frenzied thinking, but typically the pattern is this.

| | |
|---|---|
| *The Ruse* | My pursuers imagine I'm holed up here in perpetuity, so I shall outfox them by leaving. |
| *The Bluff* | But if they guess that I guess that they've guessed I'll stay put, they'll expect me to leave, so I'll stay put. |
| *The Double Bluff* | But if they guess that I've guessed that they'll guess that I guess they'll guess I'll stay put, they'll expect me to stay put, so I'll leave. |
| *The Treble Bluff* | But if they guess that I've guessed that they'll guess that I've guessed that they'll guess that I guess that they'll guess I'll stay put and thus leave, I'll outfox them by staying put. |

## Death

By the time the *Quadruple Bluff* is reached, the mind has arrived at such a pitch of agitation that, as a matter of course, it begins to wonder whether sanity itself is not just another form of lunacy. This state, often mistaken for a Zen-like detachment, is actually a bit of a nuisance since it leads to upsetting actions of a random nature such as the creation of vast bas-relief maps of the old Soviet Union using tins of whole baby carrots. Therefore, if you should ever find yourself staring down at some tins of whole baby carrots and wondering whether the Ural Mountains wouldn't be better represented if they were placed on their side ... No, on second thoughts, it doesn't matter.

# 59. THE TROUGH

Oldford Road, Welshpool/Y Trallwng, Montgomeryshire/Sir Drefaldwyn

**NEED TO KNOW:** According to the inscription, this particular trough was erected in 1910 in memory of Charles Edward Howell by his brothers and sisters, and I suppose there's no reason to disbelieve it. After all, with Edward VII on his deathbed the Howell siblings are hardly likely to think it an appropriate moment to play some sort of elaborate joke on the empire. Furthermore, their memorial to their departed brother – unlike so many that, at best, have mere aesthetic value – also works on a practical level, *viz.*, as a drinking vessel for large animals (cattle, horses, tall goats, Visigoths etc.). Just in case this secondary function is lost on the audience, the inscription ends: 'Have pity on the animals' (though oddly no specific mention of Visigoths is made). Of course, back in 1910 the word 'trough' would have been sounded to rhyme with 'cough'. The pronunciation we use today was introduced in 1918 by infantrymen returning from Belgium who had got into the habit of using Walloonian inflections when attempting what were, in those days, common English words.

**ADVANTAGES:** In today's farming-that's-a-thing-of-yesteryear-isn't-it Britain, you're unlikely to be troubled in the countryside by anything resembling an animal, so carefully scoop out the moss, lie down, re-apply the cryptogamous growth to your supine body, and relax.

**HAZARDS:** The Visigoths, thought to have been dead for hundreds of years, have recently been observed on or near the Welsh border in ones and twos. There's no reason to panic just yet, but you'd be advised to stay apprised of the latest news by listening to the regular updates on local radio stations.

**LOCAL KNOWLEDGE:** If you time your visit here just right, you may be able to catch Jimmy Cricket's show after a good morning's hiding, since he often makes it to the Town Hall at Welshpool for an afternoon gig. Furthermore, the acutely friendless can sign up to Jimmy's 'famous birthday book' – simply enter your name, address and birthday at his website and Jimmy will send you a birthday card free of charge. Not just a wonderful and sympathetic performer but a loving human being.

**FREE FOOD:** Have pity on the animals: don't eat any you find here.

**SUPPLIES:** There is a particularly good Oxfam on the High Street (0.4 miles) which offers Fair Trade foods and a 49p clothes rail.

**RECOMMENDED HIDURATION:**
2–3 hours

**DIMENSIONS:**
0.4m x 2m

**COMFORT:**
8 Plaguey

**MAP REF:**
SJ 225 072

**OS LANDRANGER:** 126

**PUBLIC CONVENIENCES:** A serviceable yet unmistakably Stalinist building in the car park on Berriew Street welcomes all comers (0.2 miles).

**IF IT ALL GETS TOO MUCH:** There's always the Scottish Country Dancing Classes (beginners only) on Wednesdays from 4.30–5.45pm at the Corn Exchange (0.4 miles).

**COMPROMISED?** Try 57. *Holly Board* (29 miles).

*Every time the camera is raised, the cunning Visigoth ducks out of sight.*

# 60. YNYS GIFFTAN

just off the coast, between Talsarnau and Portmeirion, Merioneth/Meirionnydd

**NEED to KNOW:** There is a footpath to *Ynys Gifftan* (Gifftan Island) from the mainland, but in brave new no-win-no-fee Britain there is the inevitable stern (bi-lingual) warning posted up near the crossing by the litigation-wary Meirionnydd District Council: 'Do not attempt to cross the estuary to the island', it thunders, and in case you were thinking that it would be OK at low tide, it continues: 'even at low tide.' 'How come?' you quail. 'The tidal waters are deep and unpredictable', it growls. 'So like myself', you muse. But there's more: 'The sands are dangerous.' I'll tell you, the sands were a darn sight more dangerous when they were being used to film the scenes from the cult television series *The Prisoner*, because Rover was forever bounding over them to neutralise escaping inmates from The Village (actually Portmeirion, of which you get a terrific view). Anyway, if you want to pick up a few words in Welsh while here, you could try 'Mae'r tywod yn beryglus' ('The sands are dangerous'), perhaps to use with a friend from Lampeter who has bought a faulty egg-timer that looks liable to explode in his face.

**ADVANTAGES:** With the summit a healthy 39 metres above mean sea level, even a rise in the oceans of between 10 and 20 metres should leave you dry-footed. The fact that, if climatic conditions have caused the seas to rise by this much, it means the chances of human life surviving anywhere for very long are pretty slim shouldn't concern you unduly. You are here to hide, not to take the petty troubles of the world on your already over-burdened shoulders.

**HAZARDS:** The tidal waters are deep and unpredictable. The sands are dangerous. If the tide takes you away or the sands suck you under, will you be all that much the poorer for it?

**LOCAL KNOWLEDGE:** Ynys Gifftan, in its entirety, belongs to Lord Harlech. The one building on the island, the decayed Gifftan House, has been empty for years but, according to the locals, his noble lordship might be open to leasing it out for ten to fifteen years if you've the money and a handy way with a hammer.

**FREE FOOD:** Gorse cannot be eaten as such, but it does make a decorative garnish for whatever you do happen to find around.

**SUPPLIES:** In case Nature's larder is bare, the Talsarnau post office (1 mile) helpfully specialises in foods that look good with gorse.

**RECOMMENDED HIDURATION:**
2–4 weeks

**DIMENSIONS:**
125m radius, give or take

**COMFORT:**
3 Pleasant

**MAP REF:**
SH 601 370

**OS LANDRANGER:** 124

## MAKING A QUICK GETAWAY :

**TRAIN:** Hail a train at Talsarnau station (0.8 miles) and it will stop for you. This will do wonders for your self-esteem.

**COMPROMISED?** Try *61. Arches, The New Loft Living* (18 miles).

*Who put Snowdon there? It ruins the view of the pylon. And then they complain that they don't get enough tourists.*

# PERCY TOPLIS, 'THE MONOCLED MUTINEER' (1897–1920)

> **Hiduration**: 6 weeks
> **Value as role model**: 5/10

Anyone who has heard of Percy Toplis is aware of the following facts.

i)   He led a mutiny in the British Army in World War I.
ii)  He killed a policeman while on the run.
iii) He looked like Paul McGann.

Lamentably (unless you're the policeman, I suppose), none of the above is true. However, while this might make him seem suddenly rather a dull fellow, the would-be hider could do worse than to take a leaf or two out of Toplis's book, not least from the chapter headed 'Sheer Bravado'. After all, there can't be many deserters who, using their real name, have gone on to re-enlist no fewer than three times.

Private Percy Toplis RAMC was on board the ship *Orantes* en route from Devonport to India in September 1917. This was at the very time he was supposedly leading the notorious five-day mutiny at the Étaples army camp, so you can be pretty sure that that part of his story is fictitious. Sorry about that. After several months in Bombay (as was), he was shipped off to RAMC Blackpool. It's not known whether it was living in Blackpool or the death of his father that triggered his decision to desert in August 1918.

Most fugitives would probably attempt to lie low at this point. It appears that Toplis went to Nottingham and promptly re-enlisted, a move that demonstrated a supreme (and well judged, as it turned out) confidence in the incompetence of the military police. After seeing out the rest of the war on the home front, he was demobbed, served six months' hard labour for cheque book fraud (though throughout his trial no one checked up to see if he was a deserter), and re-re-enlisted down south in order to work a stolen petrol racket. He began to live a double life, appearing in London's swankier venues as a Captain Williams. Finally bored even with this, on Boxing Day 1919 he stole an army vehicle and simply drove off.

He was arrested soon afterwards and imprisoned at an army depot near Avonmouth. Unperturbed, he responded by inviting his guards to play a few hands of pontoon with him, and in no time had pickpocketed a pistol and locked his two sentinels in his cell, waving them a cheery farewell. A few weeks later he enlisted as Aircraftman Toplis. Lucky old RAF.

On 25 April 1920, however, things took a turn for the worse. An inquest found Toplis guilty *in absentia* of the wilful murder of a taxi driver. To be fair to our man, the evidence against him was circumstantial and sometimes contradictory – for one thing, he would have had to have been in two places at once shortly before the murder, a trick even he hadn't perfected as yet.

Up to this juncture, Toplis could be said to have been a more successful escaper than he was a hider. However, over the following six weeks he managed to evade a nationwide manhunt involving hundreds of policemen. During this time, he also managed to tot up an impressive 107 reported sightings.

On 12 May he turned up in Blaina, Monmouthshire, penniless and spinning a hard-luck story to the worshippers at Salem Baptist Chapel who had a whip-round and gave him seven shillings. No doubt buoyed up by this, he made for France but found himself accosted by a policeman at Victoria station as he was about to board the boat train to Dieppe. Rather uncharacteristically, he turned on his heels and beat it. Novice hiders take note.

By 1 June Toplis was in Tomintoul in north-east Scotland, conning money out of a bicycle repair man while pretending to be an American called George Williams. That night he broke into an empty hunting lodge and, feeling a bit chilly, broke up some of the furniture for firewood. Antique furniture lovers look away now – the firewood consisted of two George II armchairs and a Louis XVI writing table. The resultant antique smoke was spotted by a local hill farmer and before Toplis knew it he was being roused from sleep by a policeman, a gamekeeper and said keeper of sheep.

Drowsy though he must have been, Toplis still had the presence of mind to go on the attack.

'What the hell are you doing here?' he asked them.

This, as you might imagine, bamboozled his prospective captors. He casually made for the door. At this point his three adversaries noticed the lack of furniture. They challenged him about this and in reply he drew his gun and shot the policeman and the gamekeeper (who both survived). He missed the farmer. In other versions of the story he hits the farmer but misses the gamekeeper. The policeman always gets it in the shoulder though.

201

Selling his bicycle, he hitch-hiked to Aberdeen, from where he took a train to Carlisle. Penurious or perhaps wishing to avoid the expense of buying a ticket, he stowed away in the guard's van. The guard discovered him almost immediately but, not realising who he was, took pity on him and they spent the journey chatting and drinking tea.

Toplis spent the following night in the army depot in Carlisle. In doing so, he was obeying the first law of hiding: 'Conceal yourself where you are least likely to be looked for.'

The next morning, which was to prove his last, the Cumbrian sun shone down on Toplis as he walked along the main road to Penrith, now posing as an army corporal. At a small Wesleyan chapel between Low and High Hesket he was questioned by one PC Fulton. Toplis gave his name as John Henry Thompson, an assertion he backed up with a driver's licence, quite an impressive feat considering the number of pseudonyms he had already rattled through (aside from those already mentioned, add Francis Edmunson, William Dennison, Percy Francis, Percy Bennison, William Wilson and, for good measure, the surnames Jones, Topley and Taylor).

Not entirely convinced, Fulton returned to the police station and checked up on the records regarding the taxi driver murder. Convinced he'd got his man, he rushed after 'Corporal Thompson' and soon found himself looking down the barrel of the fugitive's Webley 6.

Given the gunman's history, the next scene is somewhat unexpected. Toplis merely told Fulton to hop it, which thing the policeman was only too happy to do. It was this show of magnanimity that was to prove Toplis's undoing: Fulton was soon on his motorbike to Penrith to warn of the imminent arrival of the merciful desperado.

The Home Office was informed, and doubtless it was from that quarter that the order to shoot-to-kill was given. Toplis was ambushed. A short gun battle ensued and, well, that was that.

> **Lesson**: It's all right to go on the run but try not to shoot at people if you can help it because sooner or later the police are going to get really hacked off and finish you off in a hail of bullets, or something like that.

# 61. ARCHES, THE NEW LOFT LIVING

**Pont-y-Pair Bridge, Betws-y-Coed, Caernarfonshire/Sir Gaernarfon**

**NEED to KNOW:** A variation on that much-loved hiding standby, the under-the-bridge haunt, this nook of unfoundness confuses the nonce out of search parties by not being under the main arch of the crossing – under which flows the Afon Llugwy (lit. 'river of lugworms') – but a subsidiary arch (far right) that has no apparent purpose at all. Allowing free access to the crucial northern approaches to Betws-y-Coed (lit. 'a place of gambling on the results of mixed-sex schooling'), the Pont-y-Pair (lit. 'My dog's got no nose. How does he smell? Terrible.') is one of a teeming throng of bridges in and around Betws, the locals enjoying nothing quite so much as a foray or two high above a body of quickly moving water. As a result, if your pursuers know you to be partial to this genre of hiding place (or sub-genre, for those who adhere to the *Branković Classification* – see **Trends in Categorisation**, p. vii), they are likely to squander a lot of valuable time floundering around under one of the other more renowned ones such as Miners or Waterloo.

**ADVANTAGES:** Since the arch runs the whole width of the bridge, dwellers within are likely to find their movements largely uncircumscribed. However, given the comparatively low ceiling, a lolloping Richard the Thirdian gait should be assumed at all times. To get yourself into role, fix a gimlet eye on your mirrored reflection and declaim: 'Deform'd, unfinish'd, sent before my time / Into this breathing world scarce half made up', as if this somehow excused the wickedness you are about to unleash to satisfy your lust for power.

**HAZARDS:** The only sure way of getting down to the arch is by abseiling off the bridge, a hazardous exercise even if one were first to close it to motorised traffic. Since this is likely to draw attention to your proposed sojourn beneath the bridge, it might be best to wait for snow and then ski down.

**LOCAL KNOWLEDGE:** A local prince, Madog ab Owain Gwynedd, sailed to America in 1170, a full three centuries before johnny-come-lately Christopher Columbus. Scoff if you must, but there are several forts along the Alabama river, up which the prince was said to have sailed, that have been dated to the 12th century and resemble Dolwyddelan Castle, just up the road from Betws-y-Coed. Furthermore, an Alabama people called the Mandans (wiped out by an imported smallpox epidemic in 1837) were white, lived in European-style villages, and spoke a language very similar to Welsh. Don't feel so sure of yourself now, do you, huh?

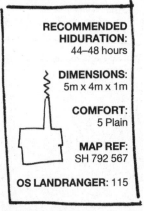

**RECOMMENDED HIDURATION:**
44–48 hours

**DIMENSIONS:**
5m x 4m x 1m

**COMFORT:**
5 Plain

**MAP REF:**
SH 792 567

**OS LANDRANGER:** 115

**FREE FOOD:** The leaves of the primrose make a tasty salady snack, though most years you may have to grow your own.

**SUPPLIES:** The Hen Siop Pont-y-Pair (lit. 'Noseless dog joke shop, some road-crossing chicken jokes also available on request') – a café and take-away – is practically on top of you, which is nice.

**PUBLIC CONVENIENCES:** Perched primly on the far bank of the river.

COMPROMISED? Try 62. *Everyday is Like Sunday* (21 miles).

*The Llugwy Cord (top right) has the reputation of being one of the most dangerous public washing lines in Wales.*

# 62. EVERYDAY IS LIKE SUNDAY

The Promenade, Rhyl, Denbighshire/Sir Ddinbych

**NEED to KNOW:** Rhyl may be the archetypal 'coastal town that they forgot to close down', as the song goes, but that's no reason for thinking it's a bit rubbish. Why, every year, dozens of dedicated fun-bound pleasure-stalkers have the best time they've ever had in their lives, or ever will have. Adjacent to the 10th tee of the Rhyl Golf Club, this dramatic opening in the floor of the promenade has been only partly fenced off by the council, allowing the opportunistic hider to descend craftily to sea level, safely out of sight of any promenaders who become so disorientated that they find themselves this far out of town.

**ADVANTAGES:** A lifebelt has been judiciously positioned at the side of the promenadial aperture. The name 'lifebelt' derives from the ancient belief that merely touching such a device could cure a patient of otherwise fatal conditions. Although there are many well-documented cases around the country of such lifebelt healings, the practice has waned in recent years and one can only commend the local authorities for attempting to reverse the trend.

**HAZARDS:** Barbarism may begin at home, but it's never long before it ends up in the sea, a reality a hider is privileged to witness at close quarters.

**ESSENTIALS:**

LOCAL KNOWLEDGE: Sir Thomas More so conspicuously plundered the concept of Rhyl for his seminal masterpiece *Utopia* that the town council of the time seriously considered suing him for plagiarism. They were eventually dissuaded by the offer from More's lawyers of an annual gift of two sloths dressed in tabards bearing the seal of the Lord Chancellor. Ironically, fifteen years later, Sir Thomas was himself made Lord Chancellor by Henry VIII – a coincidence so humorous that it became the only joke told at the King's court for two whole decades, falling from favour only with the invention of the pun. Sir Thomas' estate continues to honour the bargain and the sloths are ceremonially handed over to the Lord Mayor of Rhyl each year on The Day of the Tabards, an event that has justly become the focal point of the town's tourism drive.

**RECOMMENDED HIDURATION:**
2–4 hours

**DIMENSIONS:**
1.5m x 3m

**COMFORT:**
7 Plangent

**MAP REF:**
SJ 027 825

**OS LANDRANGER:** 116

**FREE FOOD:** They may be close at hand, but do not eat the creatures of the sea – fish stocks in the Atlantic are low enough as it is, and anything that lives in water but isn't a fish is wrong in some indefinable way.

**SUPPLIES:** There is a perfectly adequate grocers just west along the Rhyl Coast Road (0.4 miles). Nearer the centre of Rhyl there are also plenty of other retail outlets vending coastal specialities such as sticks of rock, candy floss, sailors' hats and 'your own head in a bottle'.

**PUBLIC CONVENIENCES:** Strike west along the promenade (0.5 miles).

**IF IT ALL GETS TOO MUCH:** There's always Colwyn Bay, or Prestatyn, or Abergele.

COMPROMISED? Try *25. The Fakeness of Things* (38 miles).

*Come, Armageddon! Come!*

# USING THE WEATHER

Times were when, if you were out of doors in Britain for an hour or more at a time, you could pretty much rely on it raining for some part or, very often, the entirety of your sojourn alfresco. However, with the advent of climate change and recent trends in government policy that favour the importation of cheaper, lighter clouds from so-called drier countries such as Morocco, Britain has ceased to be a place of perpetual precipitation.[1]

On account of this, the old adage:

> You may think it's jolly
> To go without a brolly
> But it is the utmost folly
> And is likely to end with you catching a chill and dying

no longer applies. Instead, the hider is left to wander the by-roads of meteorological caprice alone, aware only of the disconcerting presence of the llama of uncertainty somewhere around the next corner.

So what can be done? If foul weather can no longer be assured, even in summer, how does one prepare oneself for a climate that will not be pigeon-holed? As usual, the solution is a simple one that you really should have come up with yourself, only you claim you 'never have time' these days, what with that promotion you didn't expect and Britain signing up to the new European decimalised minute. Be done with your excuses and commit the following to memory.

### i) Take an umbrella with you anyway
By this means you can at least be secure in the knowledge that it will not rain. An unused umbrella will always come in useful as a disguise (simply open and place in front of your face – anyone you meet will be hoodwinked into thinking that you are not you at all but some other person who has an umbrella for a face).

### ii) Read the clouds
Clouds are renowned for being able to spell out words in the sky. Here are the three most commonly found words and their interpretations:

*Cirrocumulus* (good)
*Cumulus* (hmm)
*Cumulonimbus* (oh dear)

[1] Facts correct at time of going to press. Does not include Wales.

### iii) Learn to love the weather
Hail, piled up sufficiently high, makes a highly serviceable temporary hiding place – just burrow in and *voilà*!

### iv) Use the sun to your advantage
If you find yourself in a tight spot, point at the sky and cry: 'Look, the torch of the gods, it burns its fiery portents into the hearts of all who will see', and then quickly sneak away while everyone's blinded.

| SPEEDY HIDING PLACE SELECTOR | Setting | Comfort | Extended Hiduration | Fine Views | Castle Nearby | Welsh Spoken |
|---|---|---|---|---|---|---|
| 1. All Mine | R | 4 | • | • | | |
| 2. The End of Stone Row | R | 6 | | • | | |
| 3. Household in the Hills | R | 3 | • | • | | |
| 4. The New Forest Château | R | 7 | | | | |
| 5. Eeyore's Gloomy Place | R | 6 | | | | |
| 6. The Cliffs, The Cliffs | C | 2 | | • | • | |
| 7. The Clearing | R | 4 | | • | | |
| 8. Royal Crescent Garden | U | 2 | • | | | |
| 9. The Oxford Undergrounduate | R | 2 | • | | | |
| 10. Bagshot by Both Sides | R | 1 | • | | | |
| 11. The Wharf of Death | U | 2 | | | | |
| 12. The Wood at the Foot of the Stairs | U | 3 | | | | |
| 13. The Pillbox-on-Crouch | C | 2 | • | • | | |
| 14. Hollow Inside, Rather Like an Easter Egg | R | 2 | | | • | |
| 15. The Pump | U | 5 | | | | |
| 16. The Roundabout | U | 7 | • | | | |
| 17. The Hut | U | 3 | | | | |
| 18. The Thetford Crater | R | 4 | | | | |
| 19. Orford Nest | C | 3 | | • | • | |
| 20. Reedy Bed | R | 2 | • | • | | |
| 21. Railway Stairs | U | 3 | | | | |
| 22. The Lily Pond | U | 9 | | | | |
| 23. The Quatrefoil Tower | U | 6 | | | • | |
| 24. Revenge of the Fifty-Foot Herring | U | 4 | | | | |
| 25. The Fakeness of Things | U | 7 | | | | |
| 26. The Mrs Gaskell Memorial Tower was my Neighbour | U | 8 | • | | | |
| 27. The Cave in the Hill | R | 4 | • | • | | |
| 28. Not Errwood Hall | R | 5 | | | | |
| 29. The M1 | U | 9 | | | | |
| 30. Some Sort of Building | C | 3 | | • | | |
| 31. Bile Bean Hole | U | 8 | | | | |

| SELECTOR LEGEND<br><br>R = RURAL  C = COASTAL  I = INSULAR  M = MOUNTAINOUS  U = URBAN | Setting | Comfort | Extended Hiduration | Fine Views | Castle Nearby | Welsh Spoken |
|---|---|---|---|---|---|---|
| 32. Behind the Gentlemen | R | 5 | | | | |
| 33. Cavern of the Whale | M | 6 | | | | |
| 34. Your Office in the Woods | U | 2 | | | | |
| 35. Pipe Ahoy | C | 7 | | ● | | |
| 36. Priory Corner | I | 6 | | | ● | |
| 37. Robert Your Bruce | M | 2 | | | | |
| 38. Shelter of Cold Feet | U | 6 | | | | |
| 39. Temple of the Muses | R | 3 | | | | |
| 40. Welcome to Glasgow | U | 9 | | | | |
| 41. Bailie Fyfe's Close | U | 2 | | | ● | |
| 42. A Crown of Horns | I | 4 | | ● | | |
| 43. At Home with Clan Destine | M | 2 | ● | ● | | |
| 44. Behind the Goals | U | 6 | | | ● | |
| 45. Hmmm | I | 2 | ● | ● | | |
| 46. The Secret Gate | U | 1 | ● | | | |
| 47. Keith! | U | 3 | | | | |
| 48. The Benches of Hard Knocks | U | 7 | | | | |
| 49. The Turret | C | 3 | | | ● | |
| 50. The Yesnaby Battery | I | 2 | ● | ● | | |
| 51. Not Angels but Angles | C | 1 | ● | | ● | ● |
| 52. Slot | C | 8 | | ● | ● | ● |
| 53. The Shield | C | 4 | | ● | ● | ● |
| 54. The Wetness of Things | U | 9 | | | ● | ● |
| 55. Stones | I | 6 | | | ● | ● |
| 56. The Amphitheatre | U | 3 | | | | ● |
| 57. Holly Board | U | 6 | | | ● | ● |
| 58. Owain's Nook | U | 5 | | | ● | ● |
| 59. The Trough | U | 8 | | | | ● |
| 60. Ynys Gifftan | I | 3 | ● | ● | | ● |
| 61. Arches, The New Loft Living | U | 5 | | | | ● |
| 62. Everyday is Like Sunday | C | 7 | | | | ● |

# BIBLIOGRAPHY

*A Caribbean Mystery*, Agatha Christie; HarperCollins, 1964
*Bushcraft*, Ray Mears; Hodder and Stoughton, 2002
*Cranford*, Elizabeth Gaskell; Chapman and Hall, 1853
*Glencoe*, John Prebble; Secker and Warburg, 1966
*Robert the Bruce*, Caroline Bingham; Constable, 1998
*Rogue Male*, Geoffrey Household; Chatto and Windus, 1939
*Royal Survivor, A Life of Charles II*, Stephen Coote; Hodder and Stoughton, 1999
*SAS Survival Guide*, John Wiseman; HarperCollins, 1993
*The Cottager's Companion*, D.S. Savage; Peter Davies, 1975
*The Golden Warrior (The Life and Legend of Lawrence of Arabia)*, Lawrence James; Abacus, 1990
*The Monocled Mutineer,* William Allinson and John Fairley; Quartet, 1978
*The Mystery of Agatha Christie*, Gwen Robyns; Doubleday and Co., 1990
*The Road to Wigan Pier*, George Orwell; Victor Gollancz, 1937
*The Sanawarian* (Vol. IX, No. 5), various; Lawrence Royal Military School, 1937
*Trees*, Alastair Fitter and David More; HarperCollins, 1980
*Tunnelling to Freedom and Other Escape Narratives from World War I*, Hugh Durnford and others; Dover Publications, 2004 (a republication of *Escapers All: Being the Personal Narratives of Fifteen Escapers from War-Time Prison Camps, 1914–1918*, Hugh Durnford and others; John Lane, The Bodley Head, 1932)
*Wild Flowers*, Martin Walters; HarperCollins, 1994
*Wild Flowers of Britain and Europe*, W. Lippert and D. Podlech; HarperCollins, 1993
*Winnie the Pooh*, A.A. Milne; Methuen, 1926

# ACKNOWLEDGEMENTS

The author would like to express his gratitude to the following for their assistance in the writing of this book. His appreciation and thanks, if not his royalties, go to:

The Revs Carl 'Jolly Farmer' Palmer and Michael 'Mikey' Houston, Gill Nicholson, Katy 'Blades' Nicholson, Julia Castle, Carey Bowtell, Ruth Woolley, Hazel and Geoff Wills, Andy and Rachel Thackers-Jones, Clive, Shaena, Edwin, Ptolemy and Olivia Wills, Kim and Freddii Peat, Caroline and Julian Delves, Lydia 'Fit' Hutchings, Peter Pugh, Karen Efford, Damian 'Two Hats' and Renu Basher, Rebecca Stoddart and Georgina Pope, Ian Kennedy, Gail Dinner, Danny Freeman, Martin Gordon, Mark and Jude Woolley, and anyone reading this list expecting to find their name only to be disappointed at the callous disregard shown for their Herculean efforts. It's a disgrace really.

Photograph of Tibetan nomad tent by Miriam Pearce.

The author particularly thanks Elisabeth Whitebread for not, at any point, killing him.

# The History of Britain Revealed

## M.J. Harper

Do you think you know where the English language came from?

Think again.

In gloriously corrosive prose, M.J. Harper destroys the cherished national myths of the English, the Scots, the Welsh, the Irish and – to demonstrate his lack of national bias – the French. In doing so he also shows that most of the entries in the *Oxford English Dictionary* are wrong, the whole of British place-name theory is misconceived, Latin is not what it seems, the Anglo-Saxons played no major part in our history or language, and Middle English is a wholly imaginary language created by well-meaning but deluded academics.

Iconoclastic, unsentimental and truly original, *The History of Britain Revealed* will change the way you think about history, language and much else besides. It is an essential but rarely comforting read for anyone who believes that history matters.

Hardback £9.99

ISBN 10: 1 84046 769 X     ISBN 13: 978 1840467 69 7

'The most outrageous book I have ever read.'
JOHN MITCHELL, *THE OLDIE*

THE HISTORY OF BRITAIN REVEALED

THE SHOCKING TRUTH ABOUT THE ENGLISH LANGUAGE

M.J.HARPER

# Between You and I

## *James Cochrane*

'The perfect guide for those who are interested in salvaging the standards of English ... an enjoyable and informative read'
*Good Book Guide*

*Between You and I* is James Cochrane's bestselling guide to the falling standards of written and spoken English. It is the essential course in language detoxification – a valiant attempt to salvage some pearls of good usage from the linguistic dystopia of the modern world.

Many readers may be surprised to find that much of what they thought was 'bad' English is in fact perfectly good, and what they have been led to think of as 'good' English is sometimes ignorant, dishonest or plain stupid.

Paperback £6.99

ISBN 10: 1 84046 674 X

---

## Between You and I

**A Little Book of Bad English**

'A deeply-felt defence of proper English usage'
Robert McCrum, *Observer*

James Cochrane

Introduced by John Humphrys

# I Hate the Office

## *Malcolm Burgess*

A dark, edgy, yet laugh-out-loud A to Z of the absurdities and horrors of corporate life, from the pages of London's Metro newspaper.

Who, when they were six years old, ever said, 'Hey, I want to spend forty years of my life wondering what value-added knowledge capital is in a size-restricted cubicle surrounded by people who watch *Bargain Hunt*'?

Office workers of the world unite!

What makes the 9.00-to-5.30 sentence quite so gruesome? Office escapee Malcolm Burgess offers a painfully hilarious A to Z of reasons why the office has become the modern byword for servitude.

From the agony of the Away Day via hot desking, office politics, romances and parties, to the sheer terror of work reunions or conference calls, Burgess vents his spleen on the working week.

Ending with the unique Corporate Bullshit Detector, *I Hate the Office* is every stressed-out worker's essential weapon in the war against the angst of modern office life.

Hardback £9.99

ISBN 10: 1 84046 779 7    ISBN 13: 978 1840467 79 6

# It's Only Money

## *Peter Pugh*

'Money is better than
poverty, if only for
financial reasons.'
    Woody Allen

Presumably a sentiment
shared by billionaire Eli
Broad, who used his
American Express card to
buy Lichtenstein's painting
'I ... I'm Sorry' for $2.5
million, earning him
enough air miles to take
him and eight friends to
the moon and back.

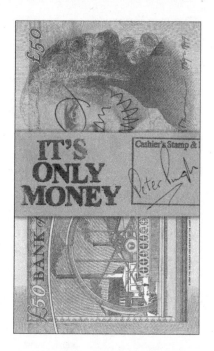

'Part of the $10 million I spent on gambling, part on booze
and part on women. The rest I spent foolishly', Hollywood star
George Raft told his bank manager. What do you suppose
Jimmy Cauty and Bill Drummond told theirs when they burnt a
million quid in the name of art? Or what courier John Goddard
reported when the briefcase he was carrying – containing
bonds worth £292 million – was stolen?

Peter Pugh's deft combination of money, history and incredible
money facts reveals that it's really not something to worry about
– its value will soon change. From the very serious to the
utterly ridiculous, *It's Only Money* tells you how to buy yourself
an £8,000 lunch, why children are a bad investment, and how
the Queen has somehow spent £5 billion in fifteen years.

Paperback £6.99

ISBN 10: 1 84046 738 X     ISBN 13: 978 1840467 38 3

# Googlies, Nutmegs and Bogeys

## *Bob Wilson*

Bob Wilson offers a champagne-spraying, riotous celebration of the colourful and highly idiosyncratic language of sport.

Have you ever flashed at a googly in the corridor of uncertainty while on a sticky dog? Maybe you've seen someone hit a gutty out of the screws to grab a birdie at Amen Corner?

The world of sport has its own language, rich in strange words and phrases, with origins stretching back centuries. *Googlies, Nutmegs and Bogeys* is an illustrated lexicon – unravelling the true meanings, heritage and evolution of sporting terms. It makes the perfect companion guide to the glorious absurdities of sporting vocabulary that continue to enliven the English language today.

Hardback £9.99

ISBN 10: 1 84046 774 6     ISBN 13: 978 1840467 74 1

# Number Freaking

### *Gary Rimmer*

'A cheerful little mix of absurdly precise arithmetic. This is a book for nutters with calculators and a lot of fun.' *Guardian*

'Gary Rimmer is the Sam Spade of number puzzles, an ambassador for freaking figures, a one-man waterfall of bizarre maths facts.' *Sunday Telegraph*

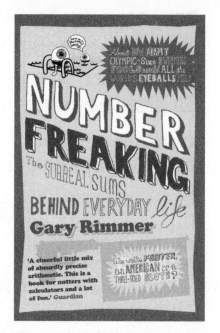

From sex and celebrity to science and sport – *Number Freaking* provides the answers to every question you never needed to ask.

- When will America collide with Japan?
- Why did Elvis really die?
- What's a decent girlfriend worth?
- Which is more crowded: Jakarta, Ikea or Hell?
- How many people on Earth are drunk right now?

Discover for yourself how far you walk in a lifetime, how many people have ever lived and how to cure world debt in the ultimate guide to modern life …

Paperback £7.99

ISBN 10: 1 84046 751 7    ISBN 13: 978 1840467 51 2

# The Man Who Ate Bluebottles and Other Great British Eccentrics

## Catherine Caufield
## Illustrated by Peter Till

'An entertaining and fascinating book about some of our best eccentrics. I enjoyed it immensely.' Sir Patrick Moore

'Mad dogs and Englishmen, laid out for public gaze.'
*Fortean Times*

'A hilarious compilation … not to be missed.'
*Good Book Guide*

Until he ate a bluebottle, William Buckland had always maintained that the taste of mole was the most repulsive he knew. But that was before he ate the embalmed heart of Louis XIV. The Comtesse de Noailles was a keen believer in the benefits of fresh air and methane gas, keeping cows tethered near her open windows so that she could enjoy both …

These and a hundred other colourful folk populate the pages of this delightful illustrated romp through the lives of some very peculiar – and very British – characters.

Paperback £7.99

ISBN 10: 1-84046-777-0     ISBN 13: 978-1840467-77-2

# The Z to Z of Great Britain

## Dixe Wills

The highly acclaimed unique travelogue of the hidden Britain of the letter Z.

Think for a moment what life is like for the letter Z. Largely neglected, it skulks at the tail of the alphabet, buzzing fitfully.

Regrettably, the same fate is shared by the 41 places in Britain that begin with the English alphabet's clammiest squib. Zabulon, Zeals, Zoar, Zouch et al. – their glories lie crushed beneath Obscurity's heel.

Not before time, *The Z to Z of Great Britain* provides an essential profile of each and every Z-bound locale. Answering the critical questions – where they are, who lives in their green bins, and what they did in the Civil War – Dixe Wills provides the ultimate guide to a Britain you hardly dared believe existed.

Paperback £7.99

ISBN 10: 1 84046 754 1    ISBN 13: 978 1840467 54 3

THE Z TO Z OF GREAT BRITAIN

DIXE WILLS

'EXQUISITELY DOTTY, YET IRRESISTIBLY CHARMING. A PROJECT SO POINTLESS AS TO BE VITAL TO OUR NATIONAL WELL-BEING.'
~ STEPHEN FRY